Guilty Pleasures

Guilty Pleasures

Indulgences, Addictions, and Obsessions

Sue Caba, Karen Hammer, J. M. Holwerda,
Cathy Luh, Catherine Rankovic, Holly Silva,
Patti Smith Jackson, and Laurie Vincent

Edited by Holly Silva

**Andrews McMeel
Publishing**

Kansas City

To order visit us at:
www.guiltypleasures.biz

03 04 05 06 07   VAI   10 9 8 7 6 5 4 3 2 1

Library of Congress Cataloging-in-Publication Data
   Guilty pleasures : indulgences, addictions, and obsessions / Susan Caba . . . [et al.]
      p.   cm.
   ISBN 0-7407-3339-7
   1. Vices. 2. Pleasure—Social aspects. 3. Conduct of life—Case studies. I. Caba, Susan.
BJ1534.G85   2003
179'.8—dc21
                                                    2002036672

Book design and composition by Kelly & Company, Lee's Summit, Missouri

"Dumpster Diving" reprinted with permission from the *St. Louis Post-Dispatch*.

Attention: Schools and Businesses

Contents

Introduction

IN THE SUMMER OF 2000, we first congregated as a critical writing group. A few months into our meetings, we wondered what would happen if we all had the same writing assignment. But what kind of assignment? We brainstormed. "Should we write about the men—past or present—in our lives?" "That's been done." "Should we delve into the turning points in our lives?" "An interesting idea, but go on." "How about essays on stuff we know we shouldn't do, but we do it anyway just because it feels good at the time?" Cathy Luh chimed in. "What, like guilty pleasures?" someone asked. An uncommon quiet fell over the room as we each considered the possibilities.

We met again a month later ready to share our secret and not-so-secret indulgences, addictions, and obsessions. Wine was poured, M&M's were served, and we devoured one another's past and current guilty pleasures. As we shared our stories, we uncovered a secret sisterhood we think extends to all women who indulge themselves—now and then—in intensely personal pleasures. *Guilty Pleasures: Indulgences, Addictions, and Obsessions* was born.

Researching this book required us to poke around our stacks of embarrassing habits and our closets full of unmentionable weaknesses. There we found the kinds of indulgences, addictions, and obsessions that we suspect many people share—but few admit. The guilty pleasures confessed herein represent the luscious and lascivious, the bizarre, the ridiculous, and the just plain fun.

We've written about going for broke on eBay, gossiping, stockpiling exotic nail polish, milking our parents for cash, and ducking full-time employment. We admit to taking almost-shameless delight in consuming antidepressants and marrying money. Among other things, the collection includes advice from a work-at-home professional on how to prepare for and secure the perfect nap. And because we've also confessed to having some unacceptable, unhealthy compulsions, we've decided to leave our individual essays unsigned.

Let go of trying to be perfect—it isn't working anyway. What's your guilty pleasure?

The Ideal Lovers: Shoes!

AFTER YEARS of curling my hair, painting my face, padding my bras, controlling my belly, shaping my thighs (finally giving up and hiding them) and shaving my shins, at last I saw . . .

That I have very attractive feet.

It was like finding and seizing on treasure.

I'd always thought that feet, because they're down there, inhabited the bargain basement of the body. Or they were like the letters X, Y, and Z, at end of the line, where things got exotic, even a little depraved, and it was better not to look. In the north where I grew up, sandals were never practical. Subways and bus stops were no place for strappy shoes. Masked by tights, muffled in socks, bound into waterproof duck boots or gum-soled sneakers or stuck in bunny slippers matted like road kill—my divinely crafted, naturally attractive feet, clear-skinned and arched "like cashews," as ballerinas say, simply waited for me to notice them. Surprise! A major lode of natural babe—discovered just when I'd edged away from vanity, and started to think that I should cultivate my character.

Shoes are the ideal lovers. They cover for you, bring out your best, make you feel self-assured, awake, and smart. And they love you back, molding to your foot and adding their character to your own. They can make you feel like a warrior, a chorus girl, a Gabor sister, an Andrews sister, a Lennon sister, a star saleswoman, or the first woman on the moon. Wherever you are, the right shoes are your ticket in or your ticket out. They know how to work a room. They exude sauciness while you keep your eyes, demurely, on the pointed toes of your brand-new red T-straps with 1⅜-inch sculptured heels or on the naked toes peeking out of your wicked black lizard-skin sling-back spikes, G-strings for the feet, that you just know *everyone* is talking about. To travel through time, I let the shoes of my life pass before me. The orthopedic shoes. The black patents with the pearly buttons. The Beatle boots. The baby blue watered-silk junior-bridesmaid pumps. My ankle-strap platforms remind me of ballrooms athrob with big-band music—places gone years before I was born. Some shoes embody melodies you can hear as you step into them. Shoes are the vehicles of dance. (A poet once asked, "Who can tell the dancer from the dance?" Man, that's obvious: The dancer has the shoes.)

The first stories they told us, the first stories they let us watch, with girl heroes, were all about shoes, of ruby and glass. So what did they expect? Why do they ask us why we love shoes?

Extorting Money from My Parents

I FIGURE THEY OWE ME. If I've figured it wrong, it's because my parents never taught me anything about money.

Ironically, Mom was a full-time office clerk and part-time bookkeeper whose scrimping and saving paid off a thirty-year mortgage in ten years and allowed our dad, a factory worker, to pay cash for family cars. During my childhood, Mom indulged herself, to my knowledge, only once, in furnishing our living room and having transparent plastic covers custom-made for the sofa and chairs.

A witness to these accomplishments, I've found myself unable to emulate them. To get money, Mom worked until she panted. To save money, she sacrificed even the simplest of pleasures and every trace of personal pride. Her white flesh burnt tomato-red, she hung from our roof all of one summer, scraping and painting the house's gutters and trim. She treated her corns with razor blades. She did the laundry in an old wringer washer that finally caught fire, and spoke hatefully of neighbors who went out for dinner and dancing.

My three sisters and I wore ill-fitting clothes with tired elastic or indelible stains, and shoes, like Mom's, of thinnish vinyl that creaked and cracked. We underwent home haircuts that seemed as lengthy and fraught as brain surgery, and, from beneath our crooked bangs, we glowered (as photographs prove) at the sparseness of our take on Christmas mornings. When we turned thirteen, Mom arranged for us to hold full-time summer baby-sitting jobs, starting the day after school let out, and smacked us if we argued, pulled a face, or were fired— as I was, at age fifteen, for yakking with my boyfriend on my employer's phone. Mom then got her coworkers to hire me to do their heavy housecleaning for seventy-five cents an hour, fifty cents if they thought seventy-five was too high, and I did this until I was sixteen and legally employable.

Mom's intentions were almost good. She wanted to teach us that we would have to earn our living, something I sort of understand. But it's too plain that she also wanted us to be on intimate terms with drudgery, and to keep our expectations low. I don't think I'm exaggerating. If she'd had any hope, or any wish, that we might lead easier lives than hers, I think she would have taught us how to draw up a budget or balance a checkbook. She only nagged us to save a dollar a week, but, given her example, we couldn't imagine what for. Daddy, for his part, pitied us and sneaked us money on the side.

The economics of our home life, minus any training in money management, ensured that I would (a) become used to being short of money, (b) prefer being short of money to working at jobs I preferred not to do, (c) idolize Bartleby the scrivener, (d) yearn to get money without earning it, and (e) immediately spend any money I got on foolish impulse items. So I've almost always been broke, but I've always gotten by, thanks to one salient sociocultural change: The kind of discipline considered normal by the parents of thirty years ago has since been renamed and criminalized as "child abuse," and is said to have lasting negative effects on children so treated.

That her spankings and groundings had likely damaged me for life came as a revelation to my mother, who is now retired and a consumer, as I am, of much TV. I know that she wishes she had been more patient with us kids, particularly with me, whose quirks and mistakes she bewailed as foreshadowings of the whole family's ultimate ruin. I remind her, when I can, that I will always carry those psychological scars. Also, Mom has since been informed that my chosen profession—creative writing! creative writing!—offers infamously low and irregular pay, making saving impossible.

Mom now happens to have money, having sold our old house at six times its purchase price and married a man rather like my late father, except that he's tighter with money, and childless. So today she lives well. She has toured Hawaii and visited Europe (taking her first flight at age forty-seven), permits herself to visit a casino once a month, and worries not about the morrow. These facts are not at all lost on me, her eldest—you know, the one she used to whip with a hair-brush, who's had years of therapy, and who takes antidepressants every day? Given that I'm the way I am, and that it's all her fault, my goal became, and still is, to get Mom, formerly a sender of ten-dollar birthday and Christmas checks, to send me more money more often.

Quitting my job helped. Tired of working, at thirty I enrolled in graduate school, and simply coming home to Mom at Christmastime fifteen pounds underweight and racked with bronchitis snagged me $500 plus the price of the round-trip train ticket.

Encouraged, I enrolled in another graduate school, and scored a car, an actual car, my very first, a five-year-old Ford with 73,000 miles. I was thirty-four. I'd phoned Mom to tell her I'd waited two horrible hours for a cab, with a cart of food spoiling in ninety-degree heat, in front of a grocery store robbed the next day by a gang with an Uzi. She drove the car up from Arizona and also paid the first year's insurance.

Even while more or less employed, I always let Mom hear about problems she could alleviate by sending me money. The theft of my backpack, with everything in it, brought forth a cool $250; windshield smashed by neighbor kids, $150; minor surgery, $100 and a nice plant; moving expenses after my next-door neighbor's car got riddled with bullets one night, $200; replacement, after the picture tube exploded, of the old TV she'd given me, $100; replacement of the microwave oven she'd given me, $50. Larger Christmas and birthday checks were forthcoming if I'd complained a lot that year ($500, $600). Two graduations netted me $250 and $500, respectively.

My stepfather has been onto my game since day one, and he grumbles, but my mother ignores him. Go, Mom! Furthering my literary lifestyle were two events worth a yummy $1,000 each: hospitalization (although insurance paid my actual expenses) and assistance in buying a new used car. Let me point out that the hospitalization was no picnic and the car was purchased only after the ailing Ford ate about $3,000 of my own money. So, you see, it's not all shameless extortion.

Now in my mid-forties, I still spend foolishly and still hate to work, but as a creative type I still enjoy adding to an imaginary book of imaginary letters to my mom:

Dear Mom:

You'll be glad to hear that I am not coughing up nearly as much blood as I used to. . . .

Dear Mom:

I learned today that when trash cans are labeled "Inedible," that isn't always true. . . .

Dear Mom:

   Did I tell you I almost got a job? . . .

Dear Mom:

   Your last letter tasted very good . . .

   And Mom's checks, now established as a tradition, continue, although in noticeably reduced amounts because my mother knows I've snagged a steady boyfriend who has a steady job. He wants us to get married. My mom has always wanted me to get married. For years now, my stepdad has taken me aside, out of my mother's hearing, and lectured me on how I need to get married. So I guess I'll have to get married, because, as they say, you can't live off your parents all your life.

Taking My Antidepressants

MY PSYCHIATRIST insists there is no seductive rush.

I am sitting in her office because of my hair, which I no longer care to wash. That, and the alluring song of the night air beyond the bridge's guardrail.

She scribbles a map, rips it from her prescription pad. This will help, she says.

Will I become addicted?

She smiles, a tolerant mother. Your brain is experiencing a chemical imbalance, she says; this will correct it.

She must be right. I've never heard of kids smuggling the jewel-bright capsules into school in a twisted plastic bag. Or sitcom stars checking into rehab to kick a Prozac habit.

Like a guide tracing my route, she describes milestones on the trek out of this cratered landscape. In a few weeks, my energy will return. Sleep will come. I'll enjoy simple things— food, books. But a pleasurable rush? Not possible.

I twist the lid and tap out a capsule. I swallow one, innocent as Alice, and begin a week's frantic ride.

Prozac shoots through me like lightning, electricity jittering the blood in my veins. Wobbly particles of thought fly off course at any distraction, unresponsive to gravitational forces.

A lead slab blocks my throat. I can't eat. The mirror reflects a bony rib cage, a knob of collarbone. In bed, I stare into the dark: alert.

My psychiatrist rips off a new slip of paper, a ticket to a different place.

Serzone slams shut the doors of perception. Bits of information—facts questions nouns numbers names—careen toward me, meaningless, and bounce off the surface of my mind like June bugs bumping against a night windowpane. I watch them bruise their wings against the glass.

She rips another script from the magic pad: a third passage.

Celexa rolls up my sleeves and barks: *Get moving!* I leap from bed. I bound to the gym. Those unanswered calls, that mail, those papers weighing on me for months, squatting on my chest like gremlins—I file, phone, pitch, and poof! All done. What was the big deal? I can't recall. I flick away pesky doubts that once assumed the size of monsters. I frown at brooding diary entries: "What if . . . ?" "If only . . . ," "What did he *really* mean by that?" Who wrote this crap? Nobody I know. I'd no sooner mull over invented slights than poke through a bag of sticky trash.

I stride through the days, hands free, whisked along as on

an airport's moving walkway, gliding past travelers lugging baggage.

Then Celexa's wicked twin flips off the sex switch. My body is no longer flesh—it has become a wooden thing. Pleasure? A memory. Caresses irritate, like sandpaper.

Next comes the migraine onslaught. Celexa crouches just beyond my field of vision and zings shafts of pain into my left temple. I'm blind. Thoughts stop, bedazzled by light and sound. Stupidity radiates from my eyeball.

She taps her pen, awaiting inspiration. We're running low on options, she says. Let's try an old standby.

Pamelor. I roll the name in my mouth like round candy. Of course, it merely corrects an imbalance. It merely restores one to oneself. It's no opiate, no creamy diazepam. But I know better.

Pamelor arrives like a warm, sudden wave. I'm lighter. I'm buoyed by salt water. Dread, that pressure in my chest, is bleached away by the sun.

I've stepped into a luscious world, like slipping into a silk chemise. I pause, toothbrush midway to mouth, and breathe the minty scent. My feet are blissful in their shoes, reveling in the solid earth beneath. A cotton T-shirt moves like satin against my skin. Lovemaking is a greedy feast.

I return for my checkup, for a refill.

She eyes me. So you're feeling better?

Oh, yes.

Appetite?

Good.

You're sleeping?

Deeply.

She frowns. You certainly *look* better, she says. She taps her pen, thinking.

I hold my breath.

Rain Dance

I DID THIS ONCE. Early June. I woke up to rolling thunder, lightning, rain. Rain in sheets, driving rain. Must have been 2 A.M. Splashing in through open windows, the rain and cool night air, cooler than the heavy humid mugginess of the evening before.

Dragging myself from bed, I pulled on an oversized T-shirt. I thought I'd close windows and mop up. Instead I went out the back and watched from the fire escape. I stood there, not long, listening to thunder and dark. Without my glasses, there wasn't anything to see but wet and water, a world cauterized by rain. I went down the metal stairs, barefoot and in my T-shirt. I went down to the backyard of the building complex, and in the middle of the storm, I did a little girly-Lear jig, a hoo-ya dance for the storm, skipping and circling, raising my arms to the sky, my mouth open for rain, as we used to do, hoo-hoo-ya-ing for snow, kicking our feet, clapping our hands, dancing in our mothers' living rooms, chanting for snow, tons of snow, five feet of snow, snow to close the highways and shut down the schools. We did this before we grew, our minds serious, no longer teasing, fun. For this hoo-ya, I was alone, stamping and splashing and soaking wet, shirt sodden, hair slathered, feet slipping in the grass. All the world, a myopic blur of rain and night, twirled around me. I felt as though I had stepped from my car at an automated car wash onto a grassy knoll, surrounded by spraying water and mushy earth.

After a time, dripping with rain, I headed for the bathroom. I rinsed grass and dirt in the tub from my legs, pulled off the heavy sodden shirt, and tossed it in the tub, too. Toweled off. Stood in the dark. Wondered where I'd left my glasses, knowing the wearing of them would return me to the world of seeing and being seen.

Marrying Money

I REMEMBER THE MOMENT I decided to marry my husband. It was a few weeks before he actually asked me, but I knew. It was our third date. We had been to dinner, which no doubt included the consumption of our usual two celebratory bottles of wine. We were standing in my kitchen, I with my back to the counter, leaning against the sink, my arms around his neck. We were talking and kissing and seeing how our bodies fit together, though we were still in our clothes. Then he said the thing that made my heart perform a round off, back hand-spring, and full-twisting back somersault, finishing off with a loud "yippee." He told me he stood to inherit a healthy sum of money from his parents' estate.

Thanks to his father's position as chief financial officer for a major corporation and prudent investing, my future husband and his brothers would take their three-way share of, well, let's say enough money to make me shrug off like a wet blanket the next piece of news he was about to deliver.

We had moved to the couch and were in the process of

ripping each other's clothes off when he pulled back and said he had something important to tell me before we went any further with our relationship. I, panting, asked what it was. He hesitated and then confessed that ten years ago, after his then wife had given birth to his third son, he had a vasectomy.

"A vasectomy?" I asked with an alcohol-induced wrinkled nose. "What for?"

"We decided after he was born not to have any more children," he said.

At thirty-four, I had not given up on that carefully cultivated image bred into all us girls about being a mommy. I had thought that once I snagged a husband, the rest would be easy—the two-story Cape Cod, a golden retriever, and the perfect little baby who would grow to make me proud. I hadn't really counted on this. But then, when I looked back over my dating life, I was once willing to march down the aisle to marry a man who couldn't have children because a case of the mumps had shriveled up his balls to the size of grapes. So how serious was I really about wanting children?

"Gosh. That's a bummer," I said.

"I know. But does it have to mean everything?" he asked.

His eyes shone stunningly blue that evening; his kisses were so sweet. My future husband had muscles in his arms and shoulders that reflected something solid inside. We had talked all evening about work and integrity and the importance of family. We had touched on politics and decided we definitely pulled the same levers. I think we both had come to the conclusion that we could be for each other what others could not be for either of us. As quickly as it could, my mind—smothered in the glaze of the evening's wine and the interrupted make-out session—tried to soak up all this information about money and infertility.

"Well, could you get it reversed?" I asked.

"I suppose that's possible," he said.

That was enough for me. In a flash, I made my decision to sell out my reproductive system. If I could persuade him to have kids, fine. If not, hey, I would be childless. But I would also have a portfolio.

Food

START WITH CHOCOLATE. Solid blocks of chocolate, shaved chocolate, melted chocolate, chocolate bunnies, chocolate kisses, chocolate in any form, bananas dipped in chocolate, strawberries dipped in chocolate, fingers dipped in chocolate, chocolate chip cookie dough, cake or brownie batter, frosting, caramel oozing out of anything, coffee, coffee, coffee, four-dollar lattes, mochas, iced mochas, frappes with whipped cream, malted milk shakes chasing down peanut-butter-and-jelly sandwiches, peanut butter on apples, peanut butter on carrots, peanut butter on toast, peanut butter on spoons, peanut butter on mint fudge swirl ice cream, the soft sides of ice cream after the carton has been sitting out, the top of gooey butter cake, buttery scones, buttery waffles dripping with syrup, buttery corn, buttery fingers, butter melting on hot bread, bagels and honey-walnut cream cheese, cheddar cheese, Stilton, Havarti, Brie, feta, Swiss, lots and lots of provolone.

Living

My friend Ellen lay on the couch buried in blankets pulled up to her chin. It was ninety-two degrees inside the house, but she asked her husband to turn off the fan. I tried to make normal conversation, but she only stared at me blankly. Did her stare mean she envied me, seeing me healthy again and with life ahead of me, but not for her? Wasn't the shoe on the other foot not long ago when she visited me in the hospital? Should I be here?

My small talk and fake cheerfulness wearied her. To end it, I thanked her for helping me in life and kissed her cold forehead to say good-bye. It was the first and only time. I felt, though, it was my kiss that was cold; there were no tears of parting. I don't know why. She thanked me in an oddly detached voice, sounding as if she were underwater. The pain was drowning out the life in her voice.

Her husband escorted me to the door. "She won't face it. She won't even talk about the funeral arrangements." He cried, but there was nothing either of us could do. I hugged him, and as I walked down the steps, I noticed majestic cumulus clouds sailing the afternoon sky, beautifully mottled with white, purple, and orange. The same wind that formed their towering updrafts blew through my hair. Everything seemed thoroughly alive, the clouds, the wind, me. Especially me. I smiled in that moment and, suddenly ashamed, hurriedly wiped the grin off my face.

The Power Play in Golf

MILLIONS OF PEOPLE, tens of millions, hundreds of millions worldwide, swing the golf club with a clear conscience. In the Palm Springs area alone, 130 golf courses sprawl across the California desert like faceted emeralds tossed on a piece of burlap. All those tanned, relaxed folks in visors and knit shirts with a crest or a tiny polo player or a miniature shark over the left breast relish every minute on the course as an escape from the real world. This golfer is not one of them.

At $30 to $200 a pop, money is one reason. Lots of people say they like golf because they enjoy walking outdoors. For free or for a few bucks, my husband, Bill, and I can hike any number of parks, natural preserves, and conservation areas. Moreover, we can take the time to focus our binoculars on the swooping feathered flashes of color that populate the skies without concern for "slow play." Also, we needn't be on guard against getting beaned by dimpled projectiles whacked hard enough to crack our braincases.

The impact on the environment is another issue. Some

reports state that golf courses use seven times the chemicals that average homeowners apply to their lawns. Not to mention the water usage, although many courses try to recycle. I always suspect that where there now is man-made terrain, hand-planted flowers, and manicured grass, forests, meadows, glades, or farmland once flourished.

Time is another problem. A round of golf is supposed to take four hours, but, let's face it, it's always longer. Factor in the trip to the course, warm-up drives and putts, and lunch, and we are talking at least five hours. Don't I have other things to do? Books to read? Causes to volunteer for? Friends and family to visit? Political candidates to stump for? Not to mention the groceries, the laundry, the bills, the yard?

And what about my image! I didn't take up golf until I met Bill in middle age. For years, I had considered golf to be an activity for mindless retirees, elitist rich people, and elitist rich people wanna-bes. I cringe every time I admit to people, especially friends from my younger days, that I play golf.

When I started playing over ten years ago, I played because of Bill. Simple as that. Golf is his passion. He reads golf books and magazines. He regrips the clubs himself. His one indulgence is a golf club membership. Besides, it is the only leisure activity at which he beats me. He begins the end-of-the-week *New York Times* crosswords; I finish them. (So much more challenging to work around *his* answers. For example, the clue was "clan symbol." The answer was "totem." Bill put "sheet.") Out of a thousand sets of tennis he and I have played, he has won two.

Lately, as I am finally breaking 100, I realize that I am getting pleasure from the game itself. I always treasure the time walking and talking with Bill, with nothing more important to decide than which club to use. I continue to admire his smooth swing and consistent stance and his ability to read the terrain.

Now, when I line up my shot, a sense of focused serenity comes over me. I have a plan of how I want to get the ball from here to there. My body can feel the rhythm of the swing: how my shoulders will turn, how my hips will pivot, how my weight will shift. When it happens as planned—a crisp thwack followed by a soaring ball in a perfect arc—I burst with happiness. At the end of a shot, I look down and am amazed and delighted to see my right leg slightly bent and balanced on the toe, just like the guys on TV. This flicker of competence—breaking 100 still leaves me some 30 strokes over par—is inexplicably thrilling. My dearly held beliefs about myself—that I'm a fiscally responsible, tree-hugging, habitat-preserving, time-efficient, small *d* democrat—are compressed into a teeny space in one far corner of my brain.

I haven't clued Bill in on my "change of heart." Every time I lean over the gorgeous, flower-bordered first tee box to place my ball, I tilt my head up, smile sweetly, and say to him, "See what I do for you, dear?"

Jewelry Jones

LAST SATURDAY, I drove to Flat River, Missouri, to shuffle for two hours from tent to tent at an open-air rock and mineral show. I never miss a rock show or rock swap that I can get to. Some of them last all weekend, from Friday through Sunday, and I attend each day, following the same path between the tables, eyeing every item: colorful mineral specimens, semiprecious stone beads, loose gems. I do this because, at these events, ingredients for jewelry are sold directly to the public at prices far below wholesale.

It so happens that rock and gem dealers are almost always men. If they are under age fifty, they wear baseball caps, sleeveless black T-shirts, and hand-cast eighteen-karat gold-nugget rings set with huge black opals or fire agates. The older dealers wear cowboy hats, short-sleeved dress shirts, and Texas-style bolo ties of turquoise and Taxco silver. "Yep," one might say, seeing my eyes catch on an attractive bit of merchandise. "That there is that double-A-grade sugilite, what they call gel sugilite. Cabbed it myself. Make a nice ring there."

Otherwise a fairly normal female, it seems I can't help but encumber myself with bracelets, dangly earrings, one or more necklaces, scads of rings, and beaded ankle bracelets, all at the same time. I try to remind myself that here in the United States, such a display borders on tasteless. But it signals to the rock dealers that even though I'm a girl, I can and will talk serious rocks. Yep, I've got the jewelry jones. And it made me a beader. Beaders are almost always females. I "bead" with beads of carnelian, jasper, onyx, wonderstone, riverstone, amethyst, azurite, agate—the whole semiprecious rainbow— plus glass beads, too, and gold and silver ones. I am not a professional. I don't want to sell any of my jewelry. I could hardly bear to part even with the few items I've given away. I just want to be happy.

Some undiscovered but famished piece of my soul feeds on rocks, jewels, and fossils. It always has. As a kid, I collected rocks from gutters and road shoulders. In my teens, I wore rhinestones to school. In my twenties, I amassed more than 400 pairs of cheap but witty earrings. Then, one day, I threw out 330 of the pairs. There followed a decade or so during which jewelry was not important. At the lowest point of my life, I sold all but 11 of my rings for scrap. Then, about a year ago, realizing that a girl can never have too much jewelry, and needing an affordable way to get it, I started crafting my own. It isn't hard to do. You need a wire cutter, wire, three kinds of pliers, a bead board, instructions, and beads.

Because rock shows are so few and far between, I also purchase beads from hobby shops and from eBay merchants named Beadlady, Beadcrazy, and Garden of Beaden. At this very moment, I await delivery—oh, I hope they'll come today—of one strand of red jade cylinder beads, two strands of blue aventurine rectangle beads, one strand of emerald-green aventurine diamond-shaped beads, one strand of 2 mm lime-green peridot rounds, a packet of 100 sterling silver 3 mm rounds, one strand of blue lace agate 4 mm rounds, two strands of 4 mm garnet rounds of AAA quality—clear as red wine—and a string of 12 mm doughnut-shaped beads cut from picture jasper. My goal is to fashion this thirty-two dollars' worth of raw materials into jewelry not even worth stealing.

I already own perhaps sixty homemade bracelets, a score of homemade necklaces. My bead board, tools, and bead containers constitute a sort of riot on and beneath my kitchen table and comprise the one mess in the house that I can look upon with love and satisfaction.

Whenever I finish a piece, I am infatuated with it and wear it all day. When I wore the very first anklet I ever made, I hopped down the street on my undecorated leg so I could hold up and admire the other. My latest creations hang from doorknobs all over the house. Each strand or bag of beads I buy, even before I open it, is marveled over and adored—by myself. Friends feign interest. I begged my boyfriend to go to the Flat River rock swap with me. He called me "a strange little woman."

And when I am not mooning over beads, pining for new ones, or evaluating and actually buying them, I am toying with some of the thousands of beads I already have, in order to come up with a viable design for yet another piece of jewelry. Using up my beads gives me a reason to buy more.

It is not lost on me that stringing beads is traditionally a therapy for crazy people, and that, outside of rock shows, bead addiction can be ruinously expensive. Beaders know that $88 is the going price for a sixteen-inch strand of Siberian charoite barrel beads, colored a rare, throbbing purple marbled with white like good steak. Last Sunday, at a hobby shop, I spent $52.09 on beads. Monday at a craft shop, Crafts and More (but what "more" could anyone want?), I bought nine dollars' worth of beads. This morning I mailed a check for $27.11 to an eBay bead dealer. But I can also buy a hank of 4,000 glass seed beads for a buck and a half. And once, at a yard sale, I secured two full pounds of real cultured pearls, stuffed into a plastic bag marked $1.

No matter how much I lecture myself ("You don't need more beads," "People in India drill holes in these beads for two dollars a day in dreadful factories," "Do you realize you just put fifty-six dollars' worth of beads on your charge card? Might you—might you *just*—be *out of control?*") the bead in me—oh, there has to be one, an inner jewel, for which the worldly ones are mere scale models or metaphors—chooses beads. Yesterday, I made a necklace of giant rainbow fluorite nuggets set off by sterling silver beads. It is insanely gorgeous, and too heavy to wear.

Surrendering to (Cinnamon Roll) Desire

YOUR YIELDING FLESH—perfumed with scents of cinnamon and cloves and vanilla—tempts me. I am alone and you promise comfort. You are insistent, I cannot resist. I taste your sweetness with a tongue tentative at first, then eager. You swirl in upon yourself, a mystery. Gently, I explore.

How to describe your essence? You are warmth, a gathering heat that draws me inward. You are spice, the elusive lands of a distant past. Your fragrance is a memory that teases and escapes me.

You uncoil beneath my fingers. They bear your flavor. You open to me. I linger. I do not want this pleasure—rare, illicit—to be too soon ended.

I withdraw and drink, to wash away your taste. Still, you are warm and within reach. I know the center of you now, and it is lush and dark and deeply sweet. I cannot escape you. You are a melting core, dissolving sweet and pungent. I devour you. You are mine and I am yours.

On Not Being a Mother

YESTERDAY I PARKED my Toyota, scooped three parcels (two gifts, one return), from the passenger's seat, then walked into the post office. I waited in line briefly, paid, pocketed my change, and was back to the car within minutes.

Through the windshield, I saw that the woman who'd pulled in ahead of me was, well, I won't say she was *struggling*, but she was still going through the many motions of getting her infant out of a backseat baby-carrier contraption and into a pastel shoulder-sling contraption.

I drove away, blissful.

The next day, I went on a long morning walk. As I passed by the private elementary school in my neighborhood, a middle-aged father was helping his two young sons out of a minivan and escorting them into the school. One of the boys was emitting piercing shrieks, arching his back, and hurling himself repeatedly at his father's knees. Front doors of nearby houses opened, faces poking out with furrowed brows and looks of concern, then embarrassment.

I chugged along happily, knowing this would never happen to me.

I've only recently come to the decision not to have children. Knowing I will not be a mother allows me to enjoy the presence of a child without having to engage in an emotional or intellectual debate about having one.

It also allows me to gloat.

It's not that I'm making fun of the man with a child's tantrum on his morning roster.

And I do not think it is mean-spirited to enjoy the speed with which I can get in and out of the post office.

I'm simply noting, and appreciating, what I haven't got.

I flew to California with my husband shortly after we were married; there was a long, late-night layover in St. Louis. All the passengers looked as weary as I felt except for a four-year-old girl spinning in circles and singing. Her young and attractive mother seemed, understandably, more undone than the rest of us. When we all finally boarded the plane and made it to San Francisco around midnight, the husband/father of this mother-child team was waiting for them.

He went ape over her.

The child.

He scooped up the little girl and swung her around and made her giggle wildly and otherwise acted as if she were returning from a trip around the globe. The pretty and exhausted wife/mother, a blank stare on her face, tooled behind them with the stroller as she wheeled toward the luggage drop. I don't think she even got a peck on the cheek.

I watched this and thought: "No way."

Sure, a child should have a great relationship with Dad, and a child's needs come before an adult's, and perhaps it was nice for the mom to go off duty. But the thought of enduring a grueling plane trip with a hyper toddler only to be ignored? I just don't think so.

I gratefully absorbed the you-must-be-so-tired's from my husband, along with his arm around my shoulder and his offer to drive to the hotel and the smooch on the cheek for no particular reason.

By not having children, I am told by friends, I am missing out on a certain type of love. Because of this, psychological texts say, I may never truly mature. All seem to agree that I'll retain an inherent selfishness that mothers shed in the delivery room.

And, as a childless woman, I should never deign to think I have the common sense or childhood memory to offer any thoughts about children to a friend who is a mother. I do, however, have a societal obligation to help raise total strangers in the village. These kids are, after all, my future politicians and doctors—or hooligans, if I don't agree to pitch in. At the very least, I am to extend a tolerant smile to the affluent couple in a nice restaurant whose child is ruining my dinner.

With this kind of guilt trip, it seems inevitable that I would, in turn, feel smug when I am witness to the many inconveniences of parenthood.

Luxury Driving

STRANGELY, I never knew I needed dashboard finesse until I was hit by a bus. My little Honda CRV didn't have much of it. It didn't curve out to gracefully connect with a center console. Come to think of it, there was no center console, and I was fine with it. It must have been the impact.

I was on my way to work, telling my passenger about the new piece of custom furniture my husband and I were waiting to be delivered, when an eighteen-wheeler that had stopped in the right lane waved a school bus (empty of children, thank God) into my lane. My passenger and I survived the experience with only bumps and bruises (me) and a broken leg (her). After a firefighter helped me out of the car, tightened a C-collar around my neck, and escorted me over to the side of the road, where I watched my friend being pulled from some very messy wreckage, I realized I had options. I could take what they would give me for my sensible four-year-old and paid-for Honda that was just totaled—crushed-in yellow—and purchase a vehicle along the same lines.

Or . . . or . . . I could milk it for all it was worth: declare it impossible to travel without the benefit of steel encasement and airbags that surround you like bubble wrap on impact; then go out and get a luxury automobile the likes of which I never, ever, thought I would own.

I now drive a 2002 Volvo V70 XC Cross Country. Loaded, as they say.

My husband and I considered other cars. A few days after the accident, I actually drove a moderately priced Mazda Tribute SUV. Nice. Smooth and roomy. It had the side airbags, the crush-resistant steel. But it also had a flat dashboard with an unreachable instrument console much like my Honda. Not much finesse. Didn't I, who had been through so much trauma, deserve better?

The brochure states: "The Volvo designers decided that there would be no compromises in the comfort or luxury of the Cross Country cabin." I personally would like to round up those designers and kiss each one of them on the lips.

When I get into my new Volvo after my husband has driven it, the seat automatically adjusts back to my setting. On cold mornings, my buns stay warm on the heated seat with the adjustable lumbar support. I can control the radio, programmed to my favorite stations, from two little buttons on the leather-wrapped steering wheel. Of course, I also can enjoy a CD or a tape in surround sound. I'm never too hot or too cold or sneezing, because I have "a sophisticated Dual

Zone Electronic Climate Control System with a built-in filter that removes pollen and dust from the air." Within easy reach on the sweetly designed Euro-gray console are two little temperature dials, one for me and one for my passenger. Also on that console is a little door. Push it in and out pops an adjustable cup holder just the right size for the Volvo travel mug Karl, the salesman, gave me. For a little tactile treat, I can rub my finger along the smooth simulated wood grain on my door panel.

As a quiet engine powers me down the road, I sit back and enjoy the smooth way my car handles every bump. I feel like Jane Jetson riding on air to the mall. When I want some more of that air, I touch the button that controls the moon roof. It slides open quietly.

How I lived without "all-wheel drive with viscous coupling and integrated 4-wheel traction control," I'll never know. But I am told that no matter how wet the pavement, my Pirelli Scorpion S/T tires will enhance my driving experience. Generally, I'm a sucker for "enhanced experiences" of any kind. Driving ones included.

Shopping ones, too. So get this. In the back of my new 2002 Volvo V70 XC Cross Country is a secret compartment I can reveal when I'm ready to pack in a load of groceries. Inside this compartment are hooks, netting, and a cute yellow springy cord that will hold my purchases in place. I always found it unsettling when the cantaloupe or the pickle jar escaped its bag and rolled around the back of my Honda. I imagined the worst. Bruised fruit. Broken eggs. Shattered jars oozing salsa. Those days are over. Now, I can make turns with confidence no matter what I'm bringing home. It makes me positively giddy.

There's just one little caveat to this undeniably logical choice of vehicle. Of course, it's the money. It takes a week's worth of my monthly salary to afford this car. Like everything else my husband and I have purchased lately—from the Ethan Allen dining-room furniture to the flat-screen television to the unbelievably wonderful Maytag Neptune with the stainless-steel wash basket that tumbles clothes clean without agitation—my new Volvo is just a little past our comfortable price range. I think we feel that if we want the cool stuff in life, we have to get it now. I don't think we're alone.

I'm forty-three. I remember twenty years ago working around women who were the age I am now. One actually declared herself "a quality seeker." Coincidentally, she drove a Volvo (I drove a Chevette at the time). It was the eighties, a time when the older baby boomers were hitting their mid-thirties and wanting nice stuff. Then, we called this group of conspicuous consumers Yuppies. Well, being at the very tail end of the boomer generation, I was young and naive enough to think that you actually had to wait to be financially ready for the luxury car, the designer furnishings, the latest electronics. Wait? Ha. What for? Just don't add it up. Then you won't know how broke your taste is making you, and the knowledge won't get in the way of enjoying your purchases and looking fashionable in the process.

So here I go. Secure behind the wheel by three-point inertia reel, automatic pretensioner seat belts, I'm ready to grab hold of the leather-trimmed gearshift knob, put the five-speed Geartronic auto/manual transmission into drive, turn up the audio system, and cruise into middle age. Avoiding the buses, of course.

Crossword Puzzle Injection

I AM LATE. For work, for the symphony, for a dentist appointment. Professional journals pile up. Salad makings spoil in the vegetable drawer. Unanswered E-mail queues up. But you can find me hunched over a crossword puzzle (Thursday through Sunday of the *New York Times,* preferred).

I get a little buzz, like a hit of oxygen or espresso, each time I find the mot juste, for straightforward clues like "cartoon ape of the eighties" (Magilla), or ambiguous clues like "It helps many machines run" (MS DOS), or punny clues like "First offer?" (Cain—off, as in murder, get it?).

I can almost hear a whir in my brain when the answer comes, like the tumblers clicking into place on a combination lock. Each clue opens the way for the next, and I keep on and on, lost in my own 15-by-15-square world. Most weekday *Times* puzzles have about 125 clues: 125 epiphanies, 125 *aha*'s. I guess I'm just—what's the word for it?—oh, yes, hooked.

Scheduling Naps

LET'S SEE. I could evaluate the challenges and opportunities of the current business climate. I could analyze the company's earnings before interest, taxes, depreciation, and amortization. Or, I could . . . nap.

In the macho corporate world, the very concept of napping elicits sneers. Hard-driving corporate strivers don't even like to admit that they need to sleep at *night*. But not everyone preens about their stamina. Latin cultures understand the precious siesta, the critical catnap, the Rx of rest. So do I.

Napping is the central indulgence of working at home. While former coworkers scan spreadsheets, I am napping. While others endure the drone of interminable meetings, I am napping. Then, while they swallow coffee to soldier through the afternoon, I can be found at my home computer, productive and refreshed from my illicit furlough.

Are you new to the work-at-home world? Let me guide you through the art of the Business-Day Nap.

Schedule your snooze with the same care with which you'd

orchestrate a committee meeting. The safest naptime falls in the halo surrounding noon, when people in tall office buildings are least likely to telephone or to expect you to answer.

Barricade the bedroom door against the worries of your work. Unplug the phone. Don't fret; if it's an emergency, the caller will summon the police.

Next, don ceremonial dress. In my case, it's soft pajamas. Yours may be sweatpants or a much-laundered, beloved T-shirt.

The nap itself is a practiced skill, like diving. Position yourself, then fall. Or, like a swimmer, relax your grip on the riverbank and savor the lovely drift.

Your thoughts will gallop like big dogs in a boundless yard. Let them loose.

Memories will wash and recede. Forget them.

You may hear words spoken by an unknown voice. Let the idle babble spill along inside your head, stringing words together in inane loops. Supply-chain management improvements oovements mooove unum. Third-quarter results, squatter ults, patter totter otter. Let it fade.

Tiring, you may catch a thought's tail, as the fisherman grasps for a mermaid's fin. She'll vanish, though, dissolving into sparkling spray. Let her go.

Images will appear, pulse and pirouette. Let them come: A woman, reaching. A hillside's slope. In a crowd, a child vanishes. Glass figurines—then a long hallway, a downward path, a journey into the mysteries of daytime sleep.

Self-Help Books

I AM a self-help book junkie.

My bookshelves are littered with titles that begin with *How to,* and others that more subtly promise to lead me down a well-worn—but, until now, hidden—path to self-improvement. The opportunities are endless, as the most cursory scan attests:

How to Buy a Car. Romance on the Run. The Complete Home Office. How We Die (not self-help—the *How* confused me). *The Relaxation Response. Easy Lawn and Garden Care: How to Maintain Your Yard and Save Time and Money. How to Garden in Containers. How to Plan and Remodel Attics and Basements. Playhouses You Can Build Yourself.* Two copies of *The Seven Habits of Highly Effective People* (both in like-new condition). A book by Oprah's cook. A book by Oprah's personal trainer. Two books by Oprah's personal strategist. *Eat More, Weigh Less. Work Less, Make More.*

Needless to say, the vast majority of these books have not been completely read. My home office is not planned for maximum efficiency. I have no deck, my child has never had a playhouse, and my container garden consists of two pots on the front porch that sport a seasonal variation of pansies and chrysanthemums, all allowed to linger far beyond their natural life spans.

I was, I guess, attracted by the potential these books represented at certain stages of my life—a thinner me, a richer me, a more efficient me, living in a better house with a better car and a more romantic marriage. If I lined them up by date of purchase, my bookshelves would be a time line of my hopes, ambitions, fears, and fantasies.

There is my perennial quest to do more with my writing: *Understanding Fiction. On Becoming a Novelist. The Writer's Journey. Writing the Modern Mystery. How to Write a Mystery. The Passionate, Accurate Story. The Complete Guide to Writing Nonfiction. How to Write a Screenplay. Writer's Guidelines. Writer's Market. The Well-Fed Writer.*

The guest-room bookshelves are filled with beautiful picture books bearing witness to my yen for a lovely garden. I stopped acquiring gardening books when I realized that, to me, the word *garden* is a noun, not a verb. As in, "I like to walk in a garden. I do not like *to* garden." See, these books did teach me something about myself.

I have my practical side, as evidenced by *The Financial Peace Planner: A Step-by-Step Guide to Restoring Your Family's Financial Health* (started this, was exhausted by the very thought of making a budget) and *Value Investing* (purchased during a fantasy that I would someday have money to invest and would do it myself.) My lack of investments is easily explained by a series of books on acquisitions: *Buy Art Smart. Classical Chinese Wood Furniture. Caring for Your Collections: Preserving and Protecting Your Art and Other Collectibles.* Buying, I've found, is a much easier skill than saving.

My all-time favorite self-help book is *Speed Cleaning— Clean Your Home in Half the Time or Less.* My copy is well thumbed and I now know the basic process of cleaning a bathroom—inside of fixtures, outside of fixtures, floor, and out the door. (The most important lesson, however, is at the back of the book: how to hire a good cleaning person.) This book pairs nicely with *Simplify Your Life: 100 Ways to Slow Down and Enjoy the Things That Really Matter.*

Motherhood opened up a whole new field for self-help and improvement. Starting, of course, with *What to Expect When You're Expecting.* Becoming a parent guarantees a lifetime of self-help subcategories. You can focus on improving yourself as a parent (*Now What Do I Do? A Guide to Parenting Elementary-aged Children*) or on improving your child (*My First French Word Book*—I thought I would have time to learn and teach French in addition to working and changing diapers). If your stress level isn't already high enough, you can compare your child's development to the so-called norm: *What Every First Grader Should Know; What Every Second*

Grader Should Know. By third grade, I figured if he should know it, he did—and if he didn't, I didn't want to know about it.

Here's a great kids' subcategory—activities to do together. These books include projects that I never, in a million years, would have dreamed up. Take *Kids' Holiday Fun: Great Family Activities for Every Month of the Year* (how to make a pencil holder by gluing alphabet pasta on an empty jar or can—estimated time, forty-five minutes, involving pasta, enamel spray paint, glue, and newspaper. My personal favorite is a book suggesting I string a series of wrenches together into a xylophone. We bought a guitar.

My shelves don't hold much in the way of the *Women Who Love Too Much* genre. Until recently, that is. Married for fifteen years, I'd thought I was all too familiar with my patterns in love, and that they were beyond major alteration. My husband, however, wasn't on the same page. I've recently acquired *Relationship Rescue, The Relationship Rescue Workbook,* and *The Relationship Cure.* I actually returned one of the relationship books unread.

The clerk wanted a reason: "I decided the relationship wasn't worth rescuing," I said. She looked at me, then ticked a box on the return form: "wrong book."

I'm now reading *When Things Fall Apart, Codependent No More,* and *Conscious Divorce.* My new bible is *The Complete Idiot's Guide to Self-Healing with Spas and Retreats.*

Most recently, I bought *The War of Art,* a blunt little how-to book about overcoming procrastination and resistance—which, when it comes right down to it, is the core problem addressed by almost every other self-help book in my library. The truth is, most of these books are themselves a means for procrastination. And, anyway, I've known the secret to overcoming procrastination for decades.

Twice a month, when I was a child, Mary would arrive at our house, which was shockingly strewn with the possessions of seven children under the age of twelve. My harried mother would wait by the door, purse in hand, to escape the chaos while Mary cleaned *and* watched the kids. When my mother returned several hours later, the house would be orderly and Mary calm. Once, as she wrote out Mary's check, my mother asked her, "Mary, how do you do it?"

Mary, pulling on her coat, said to my mother, "Honey, I just start."

Toenail Polish Buzz

TART, NATURAL, ROSE CELLOPHANE. Shake gently. *Jam, pearl haze.* Best when used with base coat. *Aurora giver, brandied wine.* Warning: Flammable. *Sheer honey, gunmetal, fresco.* The thing to do at midnight. Or when someone needs to wait for you. *Orange glow, moonstruck pink, cherry blossom.* Formaldehyde and toluene free. *Natural glow, 55; violet x-treme.* Apply two coats. *Sandstone; pink-a-boo, 13.* Nails filed straight, not rounded, are best for toes. *Sri Lanka red, Ivory Coast, sangria.* Orange stick the edges and the base of the nail. *Cinnamon toast, desert frost, peach melba.* Glob and dab the wand; stroke lavishly, smoothly. *Meringue, almond torte, basic beige.* To protect against scuffing and smudging, allow nail color to dry; blue foam wedges to part your toes. Blow little breathy puffs to help. *Blue lagoon, lilac mood, passion flower.* Read something. Watch bad TV. Top with a clear coat; dollop and stroke, ten times; repeat. *Creme, enamel, high gloss, French.* When dry, cover with white gym socks. Go forth.

Assuming the Worst about People

FEW THINGS IN LIFE are as satisfying as assuming the worst about people—and being right.

Conversation in a car, following a family reunion:

MY AUNT: Ronnie was so shy at the picnic.

ME: Shy?

AUNT: You know, shy. He's only eighteen. He gets tongue-tied when adults ask him a question.

ME: Ronnie wasn't shy at the picnic.

AUNT: He wasn't?

ME: No. He was *high*.

A month later, the phone rings. It's Ronnie. He's been arrested for possession of an illegal substance and is afraid to call his parents.

Phone conversation with my cousin, whose wife says she doesn't need to join Gamblers Anonymous:

MY COUSIN: Janice is two hours late. She must have stopped off at the grocery store.

ME: Is your ATM card in your wallet?

COUSIN: My ATM card?

ME: Is it?

PAUSE. THEN, COUSIN: Maybe I left it in the car.

ME: Your ATM card isn't in the car. And Janice isn't buying groceries.

Two weeks later, their checks start to bounce.

Short on cynicism? Spend time with a teenager.

SIXTEEN-YEAR-OLD: An eleven o'clock curfew! Don't you trust me?

SMART PARENT: No.

Conversation over lunch:

MY FRIEND: Dave has gotten to be a terrible workaholic. Sometimes he doesn't get home until midnight. Sometimes he sleeps at the office.

ME: How old is he?

FRIEND: Fifty-one.

ME: Was he married when he met you?

FRIEND: What?

ME: Was he married to somebody else when he fell in love with you?

FRIEND: Well, yes.

ME: He left his first wife for you?

FRIEND: Silence.

ME: Guess what?

FRIEND: Silence.

ME: He's not a workaholic.

It's satisfying to see what others won't.

But we're all basically good people, right?

Wrong.

We're good people until we want something that we can't have. Until somebody gets in our way. Until the truth gets sticky.

Then, you'd better assume the worst.

A Bowl of Baba Ghanoush

I HANG OUT at Aesop's Coffeehouse probably about three or four nights a week and almost always order the fresh-made baba ghanoush (eggplant dip), served with hot toasted pita bread coated with olive oil and herbs. The dip itself doesn't look like much, just a bowl of light gray-green pudding substance sitting on a dinner plate surrounded by one order of pita bread cut in triangles. Mohammed, Aesop's Egyptian owner, customarily says, "Enjoy!" as he sets it before me. And so I always do, savoring its deliciously delicate herb, olive oil, and garlic seasoning, while the cool, creamy consistency soothes my stomach and fills me with pleasure. The dish costs only $3.95, a culinary bargain.

The trick to eating this dish is to match the rate of consumption of the pita bread with the baba ghanoush portion. You don't want to find yourself with too much baba ghanoush and too little bread to dip with, or too much bread and too little baba ghanoush. I practice eating this dish as if the consumption of both elements were a game of removing pieces from a board, wiping the bowl of baba ghanoush perfectly clean with the very last crust of bread. Mohammed's baba ghanoush should not be wolfed down thoughtlessly; instead, eating the dish seems to require calculation and care, the effort expended inspiring thoughtful appreciation of its tasteful merits. "You must be addicted to baba ghanoush!" laughs Mohammed as I order it again.

I visit Aesop's for other reasons besides the excellent food; it has real atmosphere, despite its otherwise dull 1950s box-and-glass architecture. Unlike most coffeehouses that are either noisy and scruffy or too much stamped from the franchise mold, it's genuinely homey and quiet here, even when crowded with college students. A mural combining several of the paradoxical tales from the Greek fabulist Aesop cover one wall. International music plays instead of rock over the sound system, making it easier for an older person like myself to read without all those thumping, howling assaults on my theory of music.

Several beautiful handmade Persian-style rugs hanging on the wall (all for sale at a good price) add an exotic touch to the scene, as well as the less valuable ones that Mohammed has spread on the floor, even though the floor is already covered with American wall-to-wall carpet. Other Middle Eastern and central Asian immigrants to my city of St. Louis decorate their homes liberally with such rugs; in fact, they've told me they'd regard their homes as incomplete unless at least one of these rugs (whether hand or machine woven) graced their floors or walls. Among Afghan immigrants I've met, I've seen them spread a rug to function as their table for meals. I once asked Mohammed what meaning the rugs held for his people, but I think he misunderstood my question, answering it in terms of value.

"These hanging here are made of silk or wool, and have a very tight weave pattern—about sixty knots per inch. A woman will take several years to make one, and you can identify what village or family the rug comes from by the pattern. They're the same as gold. They're used for dowries, too, and are passed down from generation to generation as part of the family wealth."

Listening to his explanation, I had more in mind the ancient prayer rug from Isfahan that I'd seen displayed at the St. Louis Art Museum. The caption said the rug, with its flowery border enclosing an expanse of white space in which another flowery pattern was centered, represented the door to paradise. The devotee sat on this pattern while his prayer opened the door to understanding the mysteries. I think I wanted Mohammed to say that these rugs were still woven to be metaphorical doors to paradise, but he didn't. Maybe he's too down-to-earth to care for mystical aspects, or if he does, perhaps he didn't want to share something that deep with me, as he may have assumed I was the typical Westerner bred in a rationalist culture fundamentally at odds with mystical thought. So I didn't press it. On later visits, though, I often found myself privately contemplating the wall rugs at Aesop's, imagining their warm-colored exoticism enhancing the already ambrosial taste of baba ghanoush.

College students jam the coffeehouses of this city looking for places to study, and on most nights, I'll sense a space-starved premed student eyeing my space at Aesop's. On crowded nights, I might concede it to him and go home, or I'll arrive after nine o'clock, after most students have wandered off to their dorms. After all, I have a home with plenty of space, while they don't. Nor am I there to study for a career, but just there to read recreationally, or, more precisely, to daydream over a book, often finding Aesop's atmosphere so agreeable, I don't want to read or daydream anywhere else. So sometimes I ignore the poor premed student eyeballing my table; and parking for hours near the picture window with book in hand, I watch the street traffic, sipping on tea, wasting time gloriously.

The books I bring to Aesop's are usually on subjects out of the ordinary. The title today is *The Mystery of the Aleph: Mathematics, the Kabbalah, and the Search for Infinity,* by Amir D. Aczel. It may sound as if I like dry arcane stuff, but really it's a thrilling revelation to find numbers unlock the door to infinity. It also represents my backdoor approach to mathematics, since the more common calculating treatment of that subject is almost totally lost on me. My math ignorance always embarrassed me, but a few years ago, it suddenly dawned on me that I might be able to acquire that elusive feel for numbers if I explored it with modes of thought that have wired me, the historical, metaphorical, and mystical. I may never be able to solve an algebra problem using this method, but someday I expect primes will thrill me somehow. Or so I imagine. Last week at Aesop's, I read *The Codebook,* by Simon Singh, which is heavily laden with mathematics as applied to historical encryptions. The first chapter explained that a Moslem religious scholar, Al-Kindi, was the first to discover a mathematical method—frequency analysis—to decrypt a message, the basis of his method being laid in the religious schools analyzing the linguistic patterns of the Prophet's sayings. So it only confirmed to me that my odd methodology might well pay off, although I expect I'll continue to have problems figuring my change quickly whenever I pay Mohammed for my baba ghanoush.

Mohammed changed the recipe a while back, testing it on me to see whether I could detect the change. As usual, the taste was cool at the tip of my tongue, but then it surprised me by becoming sharper, almost meatier, as it traveled back along my palate. "Did you grill the eggplant?" I guessed, after twenty minutes of contemplating it. "Correct!" and he congratulated me heartily on my excellent discernment. Truly interesting baba ghanoush has carefully blended varieties of enigmatic taste impressions, leaving little explosions of pleasure on various locations on the tongue. What taste buds get stimulated depends on his very subtle use of herbs and spices, or how he roasts the eggplant, or how much tahini or garlic he uses, ingredients he encrypts by changing their permutations daily, just enough to throw a code-breaker off. I've asked, sometimes begged, for his recipe, but that's his closely guarded secret. Sometimes he'll hint at it, but for most of the spices, he doesn't know their English words, so he can't tell me. Its aftertaste is an obsessive puzzle that keeps bringing me back for yet another crack at deciphering its delicious mystique.

Upon dipping the last piece of pita into the last of my baba ghanoush, my gaze seems compelled to rest on one of Mohammed's rugs on the east wall, a rich, deep red carpet with an elegantly simple door-of-paradise design. I bite into this last bit of baba ghanoush as I'm face-to-face with the entrance to the mysteries, and swallow just as the door to paradise closes, but before it does, I catch a pungent whiff from its garden. Fresh garlic, probably roasted.

Soap Slut

A GOOD BAR OF SOAP is an amazing thing: the small, compact heft of it. The astounding scent and the visual pleasure of its color. That you rub it all over your body and there is maybe a little exfoliating texture or a milky smoothness and then the soap foams up and you come out clean and soft and smelling good. That you can buy new soap for less than five bucks.

Okay, so I have a bit of a soap habit in which I hoard and collect. Soap takes up very little closet space and doesn't go bad. Soap is perfection.

My personal favorite is the rounded hockey-puck design, though a thick rectangle with an arch and curved edges is extremely common and a second-best bet. I avoid at all costs thin bars of soap, which wear through and become useless almost immediately.

A pleasing fragrance that's not overpowering is arguably the most important element of a bar of soap. For example, the refreshing smell of citrus might be worth enduring soap shaped like a lemon. But a too-strong musk can nullify the entire bar and land it in the trash can. The most common crime I've found in soap scenting is the sickeningly sweet fruity bar that smells like a glass of Kool-Aid. I also stay away from all things freesia, a word that sounds fresh and delightful, but that actually translates as common and purple and cheap. The idea of chocolate-scented soap confuses me.

A nice inviting color is important. Bright glycerin soaps are spectacular looking to start with and, when underwater, look like transparent jewels. Opaque soap can be equally appealing—from muddy pastels to dense earth tones. Even a plain white bar of soap can have a lush, creamy look to it. Fifteen years ago, the anomaly of a perfectly black bar of soap in my best friend's bathroom was what got me hooked on gourmet soaps.

I would never say that exquisite little cardboard boxes don't regularly get factored into my soap decisions. But even in this age of advertising, my emphasis always stays on the soap, not its container. Except for that once, when I couldn't resist the lettuce soap in the really great little tin, which I promised myself I would reuse as a paper-clip holder.

I have my favorite soaps: products that are unfailingly sublime and always seductively packaged. And then there's orange juice soap. Oh, heaven of soaps, the orange juice soap. This stuff is refreshing and makes a big creamy peach-colored lather. I order it from Canada in huge quantities.

A runner-up to orange juice soap is inexpensively sold in the mall, is bright red-orange in color, and has the scent—and somehow even the fizzle—of an orange soda pop. It's made by a manufacturer who understands there are real soap sluts out there and offers a bulk discount.

Therapy

IT TOOK FORTY-FIVE MINUTES in heavy traffic for me to get from my front door to the long gravel driveway. I pulled in and drove up to the barn, walked across the cedar deck and down the steps to the door labeled "Office."

A comforting little bell announced my arrival, which was usually ten, sometimes twenty, minutes early. I sat in the waiting room and looked through smudged picture windows. Outside, a valley glistened with the dappled light of a setting sun. Vigilant deer and wild turkey, content and grazing horses, and rustling sugar maples added motion to the peaceful landscape. A large orange tabby leapt onto the deck from somewhere below, pawed the railing, curled its back, and waited for me to open the door. It sidled in, brushing the side of its body along my shins. I took a deep breath. I had made it through one more week.

Always ten or fifteen minutes after our appointed time, Alan would burst through the inner door, apologize for running late, offer me coffee, invite me in. As I passed through the threshold and into the sanctuary of his office, he'd always make it a point to touch my shoulder and look into my eyes. These gestures, of course, were all part of the therapy.

Every week for seven years in my late twenties and early thirties, I opened my heart and soul to Alan's cognitive therapeutic wisdom. It was fifty dollars a session, paid exclusively out of my shallow pockets. But, God, I loved it.

Session one: *Alan diagnoses my problem.*
"Chronic depression and post-traumatic stress," he pronounced with confidence. He said it was my father's drinking, my mother's enabling, my brother's dying, and my angry siblings. I believed him. Why else did I always pick the wrong men? Why else was my self-esteem in shambles? Why else could I not stop crying?

Session two: *Alan puts me on antidepressants.*
"They'll get you out of the hole you're in," he said in answer to my initial protest. "Then we can start working on some issues."

Session three: *Alan gives me a "where and when" of Al-Anon and Adult Children of Alcoholics meetings.*
"I encourage you to go to as many as you can get to in the next ninety days," he said. I nodded soberly. He took notes as I talked and memorized the birth order of my family:

Timdavidlisapollystevenchristyjohn. He introduced me to the concepts of shame, addiction (others, not mine), and codependency. He told me to read *The Dance of Anger, Adult Children of Alcoholics, Codependent No More.* Bradshaw. He handed me a box of Kleenex. I blew my soggy nose.

Session four *and on and on and on:*

I railed against my parents. I mined past actions of my siblings, looking for traces of sabotage, for all the ways they helped ruin my life. "He hid gin bottles in the garage." "She always denied the problem." "They left me there with him."

Together, Alan and I connected our dots. We created links between the times the adults in my world did this or that when I was ten years old and the times I showed poor judgment when I was eighteen, twenty-four, twenty-eight. I dated an abusive, alcoholic air traffic controller? Definitely blame that on my dad's drinking. What? I pinned my hopes on marrying an emotionally unavailable workaholic lawyer whom I really had nothing in common with and whose body, to tell the truth, repulsed me? Yep. Chalk that up to my low self-esteem created by lack of sibling attention. Oh, what joy! You mean to tell me my one-night stands were related to the abandonment I felt during my tender years? No wonder I couldn't help myself.

"Do you think *I* might have a drinking problem?" I asked Alan once, just once.

"Naw," he answered, lighting his third cigarette of the session. "You're too controlling to have a drinking problem."

I didn't know what that meant, but I liked the sound of it.

The weeks turned into months, the months turned into years, therapy turned into bitch-and-gossip sessions. When Alan's wife left him, he was bereft, too undone to pick up the phone and cancel our appointment. We spent the entire hour talking about her, how she left while he was out of town, packing everything (including stuff of his) into a Ryder truck, and acting cheerful, like nothing was wrong, when he called from the road. I hugged him and wrote out a check for fifty dollars before I left.

"See you next week," he said.

"Of course," I said.

I sent a friend to him. She started hitting on him. He talked about her to me. Was that a breach of patient confidentiality? Certainly not. He wasn't telling me anything I hadn't already figured out using my growing wisdom and insight into the human psyche and the psychological damage wrought by fathers who kept gin bottles in the basement. Fifty dollars, please. No problem. Commiseration with the one I loved. How sweet it was.

On Thursdays, I saw Alan. On Saturday mornings, I went to my "home group" of Adult Children of Alcoholics, held in a third-grade classroom of a Zion Baptist Church school. There, my fellow sufferers and I arranged child-sized chairs in a circle. "God, grant me the serenity to accept the things I cannot change, the courage to change the things I can, and the wisdom to know the difference," we prayed. Then we went around the room taking turns bemoaning how this person or that person from our past or current lives refused to see the light. The definition of bliss.

During all this therapy and hugging and "learning to listen" and journaling and "workshopping my feelings" and dealing with my feelings and inspecting my ability for introspection, my mom was learning how to transfer my dad from the bed to the wheelchair to the toilet to the wheelchair to the recliner to the wheelchair to the car to the wheelchair to the doctor's office to the wheelchair to the car to the wheelchair to the bed. About twelve years after the humiliation of a DWI convinced my dad to go cold turkey on the drinking, he suffered from a stroke that the doctors characterized as "catastrophic." For the next two years, my mom took care of him 24/7. If the timing wasn't quite right for me to phone and write her in order to articulate *my issues* about how I was raised, it didn't occur to me. And why should it? Didn't Alan and the people in my group encourage me to express my feelings? And wasn't I too busy working on *my issues* to go over there to help lift him and feed him and wipe the drool off his chin?

Well, yeah.

Smoking

THE BEST PART OF IT: unwrapping the cellophane, holding the rectangular pack square in one hand, and with the other, pulling the thin red line and twisting it all the way around until the top squared off pulled cleanly away with a crinkly snap, and then sliding a fingernail, always my index finger, under the triangulated foil, peeling it back, tearing it in a clean square to reveal five butt-ends, and tossing the foil away, to the ground, usually. Once opened, thunking the pack against my hand, thunking it once, twice, a third time, to tamp any loose tobacco tight against the filters, and then thunking one more time against my fingers to shake a cigarette loose, then lifting it, pack and all, to my mouth, like the Marlboro man on TV, and with my lips, softly puckered, teasing and cajoling, teasing and pulling, one cigarette from the pack. And then, a flick and a twist, the jump of flame from a lighter, and the suck and slow drag until an ember glows and smoke froths in my throat.

Playing the Race Card

IN *SOUTH PACIFIC,* Bloody Mary, the betel-nut-chewing native woman with "skin as tender as DiMaggio's glove," takes Lieutenant Cable to the mysterious island of Bali Hai. She introduces him to her daughter Liat. Played by Eurasian France Nuyen, Liat is young and beautiful. From the beginning, her doe eyes convey total trust and acceptance of Cable. Bloody Mary sings "Happy Talk" while Liat's radiant face, slim arms, and long, slender fingers pantomime the words. Finishing the song, Bloody Mary looks at Cable and asks, "You like?"

Other images come to mind. Tuptim (Rita Moreno), gift-wrapped as it were, in a form-fitting (and form-revealing) jacket and long, narrow skirt kowtowing to the king of Siam when she is offered to him as a present. Maily, a 1920s Chinese prostitute in *The Sand Pebbles,* saying to the sailor Frenchy, "I'll do what you want. You bought me." Any role by Miyoshi Umeki as she shuffles forth in her kimono, head and body leaning in attentiveness, smile warm but not forward, hands folded prayerlike in submission.

These characters are never fully drawn. They don't have neuroses, favorite foods, or facial tics. They are quiet and demure. They are compliant and trusting. And they love their men, most of the time Caucasian, without reservation or question. As Lady Thiang, "head wife," sings in *The King and I*, "This is a man you'll forgive and forgive, and help and protect as long as you live. . . . He has a thousand dreams that won't come true. You know that he believes in them, and that's enough for you." Oh, and these girls are all Asian. The strong-willed, conflicted roles such as Ensign Nellie Forbush and Anna Leonowens are reserved for white women.

A variation of the young, beautiful, trusting girl is the young, beautiful, trusting hooker, like Suzie Wong, Kim in *Miss Saigon,* and her predecessor, the geisha Madame Butterfly. Yes, she sells her body, but only so she can support her family. That she is sexually knowledgeable and willing makes her that much more interesting. The Caucasian man falls for her and wants to save her from her tragic fate and, of course, for himself. In the end, she falls for him, too, and, because of her dire straits, she needs him more than he needs her. This is the romanticized appeal of the Asian mail-order bride phenomenon: someone sexually receptive, as the Discovery Channel puts it, and economically dependent! What an ego boost.

When I was still what psychologist Barbara Sher calls a "breeder," attracting a mate was paramount. (Okay, so I told my parents I was in college because of a passionate interest in medieval Japanese literature.) On meeting a cute guy, I'd already be looking to see if he wore a wedding band. I'd hang out in Washington University's Holmes Lounge for hours, looking to meet someone or, more often, hoping the guy I had my eye on at the time would show. I wore down-to-there hair and up-to-there miniskirts. And, with my Chinese face, I was not above using the cultural perception of the docile-in-every-way Asian female to my advantage. I wanted guys to think that, in me, they could get a sexy girl who also had the vulnerability and purity of heart of the Asian film ingenues. To a man predisposed, a shy smile with downcast eyes, a toss of the head allowing a sheet of shiny black hair to cascade to one side, and a seemingly inadvertent double entendre or sexual reference—"Oh, you know, she lives in the Loop, that street between Eastgate and Westgate, Intercourse, oh, I mean, Interdrive"—sets the hook.

I met with spotty success—most guys were still looking for the leggy blonde cheerleader—until more and more veterans started showing up on campus on the GI Bill. They were easy to spot: slightly older, slightly ill at ease to find themselves in an academic setting, smoking Camels, Winstons, or Marlboros, and wearing bits and pieces of army clothing with its black block stenciling. They spoke a lingo that incorporated words like *lifer, Skivvies,* and *mullet* (navyspeak for a dumb person, I was told). Exotic place-names like Subic Bay, Okinawa, Yokohama, and Da Nang tripped off their tongues. And, boy, was I a babe to them. My appearance tapped into their idealized memories and expectations of the Vietnamese, Chinese, Thai, Taiwanese, Japanese, Korean, or Filipino girls they had known in Asia, which had only reinforced the American popular stereotype of Asian females. It was my dating heyday: Bill, whose Monterey Air Force Institute Chinese was better than mine; Jon, who introduced me to bluegrass and Bill Monroe and Doc Watson; Pat, who refused to talk about his Green Beret experience; Chuck, on whose motorcycle we rode from Austin to Houston one summer weekend; and Tony and Harry and Joel. I was a vet magnet.

Of course, I did not live up to these feminine Asian images. No one could. I was much better. These men found out that there was a lot more to being with me than having someone adore them. I could run them around a tennis court, stay up late dealing poker, canvass for political causes, and have sex—if and when I wanted to. Some liked it. Some didn't.

In the end, I married David, who not only wasn't a vet, but also spent his draft-eligible years as a conscientious objector. He had, however, spent two years in Hong Kong(!) in the Yale-in-China program. We bred and produced Alex.

As the years and the fads went by, I became a doctor, divorced, remarried, and raised Alex. To seem smart, progressive, "with it," and agreeable, I have not disabused people of their ideas of me based on whatever their source of the Asian female might be. I graciously accept the "compliment."

"You people are so smart," an elderly patient, Ethel, told me. Yeah, me and the other 999,999,999 Chinese. When there is a delicate suturing job, it is terrific that we are so "good with our hands." In the seventies, members of the social and political counterculture assumed that the *Kama-Sutra,* macrobiotics, *I Ching,* Taoism, and Chairman Mao were all in my bailiwick. In the eighties, Alex's grade-school pals were sure that I was an expert, if not at karate and kung fu themselves, then at least on the Shao Lin Temple and Chinese monks who roamed the old West. In the nineties, New Agers would say, "You're not closed-minded like the AMA," and included me among the proponents of crystals, acupuncture, magnets, chakras, blue-green algae, allergies to everything synthetic, auras, and healing touch. I smiled and went along, liking the idea that people thought I really knew about all this stuff and finding it too overwhelming to try to explain that they were stereotyping me.

My one regret is that I tried to foist one of these myths on Alex. When I told him that all Chinese could do math in their heads, the kid who forgot how to do long division the summer after fourth grade squealed in panic, "But I'm only half Chinese, Mom."

Me and My Rifle

GUNS ARE FUN. I have a rifle, but it's not exactly like Chuck Conners's or John Wayne's. Mine's an air rifle, a Benjamin. It shoots not bullets, but .177-caliber pellets, which are smaller than some BBs, and only one of them at a time. If I fired at an actual squirrel, my pellet wouldn't do much more than sting its little heinie and scare it.

Nonetheless, I love my rifle. It's not like me to say so. If they gave prizes for moral character, I would win second place in the Miss Straight and Narrow competition. I wear bifocals and frumpy skirts. I eat balanced meals and anxiously apologize when I've called a wrong number. I'm not the reckless type. Not surprisingly, I've always held a low opinion of guns. Gun-lovers have always gotten my most scalding stares. I've voted for handgun laws and against the right to carry. My father owned a hunting gun, a shotgun, but kept it in a canvas bag that rendered it featureless and too scary to touch.

I handled a gun for the first time at a YMCA-sponsored weekend designed to teach women outdoor-type skills. Some women came to learn to sail; others, to climb rocks. Because it wasn't like me—I've always felt more like a target—I chose to learn to shoot. The paper targets we got were stamped with the National Rifle Association's seal of approval. When I saw that, I made a face. But just a few days ago, I bought my own packet of NRA-certified targets for small-bore guns like my cute little Benjamin, and I now think the NRA is cool, at least as cool as NPR, and if anyone wants me to give up my rifle, they'd better be set to pry it from my cold dead fingers.

Our class was made up of women much like myself, most of them conscious of the need, at this stage in our lives, to keep our shorts and skorts at or below our kneecaps.

Before even getting near a gun, we attended a three-hour lecture on firearms safety, about which we became instantly fanatical. Remember: Always point the muzzle in a safe direction, treat every firearm as if it were loaded, and so forth. The rifle-range instructors—there were two, in case one of us old biddies went hog-wild, I guess—had set out for us five German-made air rifles, obviously very fine, trade-named Diana. For the first time, I thought: "A beautiful gun."

The instructors explained to us that air guns use compressed air, not gunpowder, to propel their projectiles, and thus do not "kick," smoke, or stink. How pleasantly genteel! Then, with the instructors correcting our form, we each took a turn pumping up a gun, aiming, releasing the safety switch, firing the thing *(bam!),* and switching the safety back on.

"Well, I never!"

"Dang! It's fun!"

To me, the Diana felt dreadfully heavy. Pumping it up just once took all of my strength.

"She can't handle that," one instructor told the other.

"Yes, I can," I said, and poked a pellet into the chamber.

"Commence firing when ready," the instructor said.

My heart pounded. The muzzle wavered. I held my breath and fired—*fing!*—into the backstop. It *was* fun!

After four or five rounds, we were as insatiable as ten-year-old boys. Some of us had to sit down and prop our elbows on a tabletop to aim and fire, but even so, we were soon hitting those paper targets. Giggling gave way to cackling. We grew profane and spun variations on "So-and-so had better watch out!" Miss Straight and Narrow, who is always truthful, confesses that she is unable to explain the sudden development, in her previously meek and retiring spirit, of hearty good humor, confidence and ferocity, and a desire to obtain her own gun and to shoot things.

So I went home and bought my rifle. It's two pounds lighter than the Diana, but it's not a gun for sissies. I'm becoming an excellent shot. Out in my meadow, I trapshoot for target practice and fun. The pellet goes into a "trap," a boxlike thing where it stops and sticks. Nobody gets hurt. I made my own trap out of a cardboard box packed tightly with phone books and back issues of *Cooking Light* and *The New Yorker*.

I love my rifle. I even love to say "my rifle." What, don't I seem like the type? Come on over and try out my rifle. It'll make your day. And—oh, dear, but staying honest means I have to admit to it—I am the NRA.

Screening Phone Calls

"IT'S ME. My brother is stirring it up again. Wait till you hear what he pulled this time."

> —Family friend whose brother was arrested
> after brandishing a knife at his ex-wife

"Hi. Shirley here. It's been six and a half weeks since we've had lunch. I was wondering if you were available next month on a Tuesday at eleven forty-five. My second and fourth Tuesdays are still available."

> —Control-freak friend

"Ilona with Marriott calling back. Have you decided on the offer for the three-day golf package at our Williamsburg resort for only one hundred ninety-nine dollars? Please call me.

> —Aggressive time-share salesperson's third
> call this week

"Haven't seen you in a while. Wanna play tennis tomorrow at six-thirty A.M. at Forest Park?"

> —Woman who has lost every match we've played for three years

"This is Kathleen. Did you get my E-mail? I have a few questions to ask you before we can go ahead with the analysis. You can call me anytime at your convenience, or you can just answer my E-mail."

> —Investment broker dangling the prospect of retirement riches through adoption of the Merrill Lynch portfolio analysis

"This is Gary. Liz and I have to be at meetings all day Wednesday. Do you think you can work a few extra hours? Call me at home. Thanks."

> —My boss

"Hi, this is Caroline. Can you call me back? I have a question to ask you."

> —Ex-member of my investment club who is suing us because Cisco went south

"My name is Laura. Your cousin Chris gave me your number. I think you might be able to answer some questions I have about acupuncture."

> —Total stranger who is desperately looking for the magic bullet for her desert dust, avocado, gold, silver, and eggplant allergies

"This is Theresa. I need to talk to you about a health issue. I've been on Prempro for five years. I want to discuss the pros and cons."

> —Panicked menopausal friend trying to sound like she's calm

"Hi, it's Diane. Congratulations about your book. I've written a novel. Would you know any publishers who'd be interested?"

> —Someone I haven't talked with in ten years

"I'm not here to take your call. Please, *please,* leave your message."

> —Sweet-voiced, lying me, who listens as the answering machine takes messages

eBay Inebriate

I WOKE UP this morning with an eBay hangover.

I lingered too long—well past midnight—at my computer, tap, tap, tapping at the keys to protect my bid on a seductively squat green Arts and Crafts vase. If I could get my heart pounding on the treadmill at anywhere near the rate it was going during those final auction minutes, my cardiovascular health would be immeasurably improved.

For the two of you who haven't heard of it, eBay is the enormously popular on-line auction service spawned—of course—in the fertile mind of a Silicon Valley entrepreneur. With recent sales of $5 billion a year and 46 million registered users, eBay has literally changed the way the nation does business. I could buy anything on eBay, including a kidney. Right this minute—and it grows hourly—there are 1,307,818 items listed in 24 categories of collectibles alone.

To me, eBay is the computer equivalent of heroin for a junkie or a dog track for gambling fiends. Neither drugs nor gambling have ever held any allure; I've always preferred to squander my money at flea markets and antique stores. My only mindless addiction has been FreeCell, a version of computer solitaire. Now, along comes eBay, a heady mix of game strategy and shopping, spiked with the adrenaline rush of high-stakes wagering. In my first seven days on-line, I bid on twenty-three pieces of pottery. If I'd been the winning bidder in every case, I'd have spent $775.75. And that was before I refined my searching techniques and sharpened my strategy for bidding.

I am not alone in my obsession; eBay records 1.5 *billion* page hits a month. Of course, a good percentage of them are mine.

I was hooked on a Tuesday, at 11:28 A.M., according to that fateful first E-mail from eBay, confirming my registration as a bidder. My addiction was assured the moment I dipped into the index of American pottery, voluptuous vessels with sensuous shapes and matte glazes that invite a caress. Within eight hours, I was in the throes of a down-to-the-wire bidding war.

Gotta pause here—just remembered I need to check the listings of Nate at Artpots.com, to see if he's reoffering a piece I have my eye on. I was the high bidder the first time around but didn't meet his reserve. Besides, there's an auction on a little maroon lamp ending in seven minutes—my final bid was $16.75, but someone beat me by $.50. Just want to see what it sells for. . . . Aah, resisted the temptation to increase my bid, let the little lamp go for just $17.25. See, I can quit any time I want.

Alice, a friend, introduced me to eBay. She shares my affinity for those fat Arts and Crafts pots and knows how scarce they've become in the antique and junk shops we haunt. "Just look," she coaxed. "It can't hurt to look."

I was ripe for temptation. I was never a gambler. And games—Scrabble, poker, miniature golf—always bored me. Then, about a year ago, I discovered computerized card games. Solitaire was engaging. I'd get that little thrill when I won and the cards cascaded home electronically. I moved on to Free-Cell. There was more strategy involved. The thrill was more intense. There was a little animated king who sat between the cards and turned his head to watch every move I made.

Three games, I'd tell myself. Or three *winning* games. Best three out of five. I'd look up to find forty-five minutes had evaporated. I began to experience self-loathing. I deleted FreeCell from my computer. The next day, I was desolate, bored, restless, and unable to write. Checking—and rechecking—my E-mail didn't give me the same thrill. I needed something more, something interactive.

That's when Alice led me to eBay.

Just spiked up my bid on an elegant RumRill vase, creamy shade of ivory, great shape, wonderful age crackle. I was already high bidder at $13, but the red lettering on my bid list indicated the seller's reserve hadn't been met. I increased my maximum from $18 to $21, still didn't get the green lettering that indicates a "win." I want that vase! I bid higher. Bingo! Green lettering, *seller's reserve met at $24. Immediately, I felt the fool—still a day and a half till the auction ends. Why, oh, why, had I tipped my hand? Have I alerted others to my find? Will Marciamay, my rival bidder for the vase, jump back into the game?*

Make no mistake, eBay is a game. Okay, maybe it's not Doom—it just feels that way as I plumb the various levels of the eBay universe.

At first, I just clicked on my search topic and scrolled through the index of items for sale. Then I learned to search by the names of the great American pottery makers—Weller, McCoy, Fulper, Roseville, Rookwood, Stangl, and Coors. (The list grows longer and longer—the more I search, the more I learn, the more I refine my searches.)

The names of certain sellers became familiar—oldpotshop and findgreatstuff (who turned out to be acquaintances from a flea market in New Jersey), to name but two. I began to detour off the main directory to explore their listings, finding myself in intriguing cyberspace caverns filled with riches.

And then it dawned on me: Know thine enemy! I realized I could pull up an index of everything my rivals were bidding on. A wealth of competitive information was a mouse click away! *This* one buys a lot and often spends top dollar. *That* one purchases only a certain shade of green. *This* one is a serious collector of Fulper, while *that* one over there is indiscriminately bidding on pink Pyrex, floral hooked rugs, and almost any cheap green vase. *This* one, I can't beat; *that* one, I'll defeat!

From there, it was a short step to espionage. Isn't it only natural I would discern that a certain someone, judging by his bids, seems to share my taste in Arts and Crafts pottery? And that he has discovered a Brush-McCoy bowl I simply hadn't seen yet? Wouldn't I have found it anyway, even if I hadn't noticed it on his list of open auctions? After all, eBay listings are color-coded—even when you're looking at someone else's bidding history—so you can see at a glance which items you've looked at and which you've missed.

Alice thinks this may be dirty pool. I say auction is war and the most adroit bidder wins.

Excuse me. I'm bidding on an Arts and Crafts lamp, in an auction that ends in twenty minutes. I'm up against a man who bids thousands on nothing but the best. I decided to enter a high bid an hour before the auction ends, then hope to surprise the competition by doubling the amount just before the gavel falls. Yes! The lamp is mine!

Have I mentioned bidding strategies? According to eBay, I should enter my highest bid early, then let the computers dole out dollars as the auction heats up. Sure, it sounds rational—it should keep my competitive fervor from overrunning cool analysis in the final minutes of bidding.

But I fall in love with an item the first two or three times I see it. "I'd buy that pot for eighty-seven dollars," I said of my first acquisition (odd-dollar figures give you an edge over people who bid in five-dollar increments). I didn't yet know how many pots were out there in cyberspace. I got that pot—and the sixty-one-dollar bill that went with it—to my chagrin. In the world of business, this is known as "irrational escalation." I needed time to let my ardor fade.

Now I bid low at first, just a dollar or two more than the minimum, to put the pot in my index of ongoing sales. Then I watch. If someone outbids me, I toss in a few more dollars to test my rivals' commitment. Or I let their high bids linger, while I calculate my finances and consider my alternatives.

I'm looking for my heartbreak price—a slippery number that defines whether I'll be crushed because I didn't bid higher and lost, or sick at heart because I bid too high and won. I like to stage my final bids according to the competition.

And I'm not above the snipe—blasting away with an unexpected bid in the final minutes of a sale. I read about a woman—the Rambo-ette of cyberspace—who keeps nine eBay screens open on a console of three computers. She has a chair that allows her to swivel from one screen to another and bid at the last minute. *Bang! Bang! Bang!*

Well, there's more, so much more, I could tell you. But I'm loath, I acknowledge, to reveal all my bidding secrets. Besides, there's an absolutely fabulous green vase, Roseville Baneda pattern—mint, no chips, cracks, or flaking, according to the seller—that closes in about five minutes. . . .

Eye Candy

WHEN YOU LEAST expect one, when you've all but given up, the universe puts in your line of vision a guy sporting a piece of triangular cloth worn like the hybrid hat and skullcap the doo rag is. Doo rags cross the forehead just above the eyebrow, cover the head to the top of the ears, and tie in a three-cornered knot at the back. Some guys wrap specially designed skull-and-crossbones prints with extended ties around their heads, probably ordered from buycool.com.

Nothing is sexier than a doo rag fashioned from a cloth handkerchief in the traditional red, black, and white paisley bandana.

Only a sign, of course, the red-bandana doo rag puts you on alert for strong, stoic, silent, resourceful; physical self-confidence and mechanical inclinations; good hands. Masters of the inscrutable, guys like these stare at a point some yards distant, sun-earned crinkles at the corners of their dark eyes, strangers to shades. Lots of guys wear blue-bandana doo rags, but these guys usually wear goatees, and when they aren't sitting at traffic lights in oxidized vans with rusted quarter panels, they are found pulling the hairs in their sideburns and watching someone else hustle pool. Blue bandanas are best used to clean up, wipe off, and blow into; so if you see a guy in one of these, look the other way; wait for the red.

And when you see a red doo rag, you'll see lean, sinewy, tattooed biceps throttling a machine, like a power saw or a chopped Harley, or humphing free weights, his lower half sporting a six-pack, blue butterfly shorts, and Saucony's. Little in the free world offers better eye candy than this.

Eating Liquid Gold

THE TASTE is pure sunshine, a big dollop that squirts in your mouth. The texture is silk, smooth and luxurious, as it coats and then slides down your throat. The color is twenty-four-karat gold, shiny and intensely yellow.

The perfect way to eat an egg is right after the hen lays it, still warm. Crack the big end, peel off the dome of shell, and suck with a gentle and steady pressure until the yolk bursts forth its richness right into your mouth. I did that as a kid when our family kept a pet hen.

Nowadays, I toss a raw egg into a bubbling-hot bowl of oatmeal to give it a custardy flavor. I throw a raw egg into steaming rice gruel and season it with soy sauce to make a tasty soup. I crack a raw egg on hot noodles to make pasta carbonara.

I know all about the "S" word: salmonella. The USDA tells me to cook eggs until they are dry and lifeless under penalty of gastroenteritis. Even the least bit of softness in the yolk puts me in danger. Still, I choose to run the risk several times a week in order to taste the sunburst inside my mouth.

Needy Friends

GIRLS, I have the perfect drug. It is not illegal. It will not make you fat. It will cost you nothing. It is perfectly socially acceptable. It can be at once pleasantly numbing and shockingly stimulating. It has no odor. It causes no apparent side effects. Its one seeming drawback is the time it demands. But this can be a good thing.

So go ahead, make friends with someone whose life is in complete disarray. You will see what I mean.

For this prescription to work at maximum strength, the chosen friend must meet the following criteria:

First, must have an outstanding outward appearance. The friend you choose must be of middle-class means. The impoverished will not do. Their problems—trouble paying the rent, medical bills, abusive husbands, social workers threatening to take children away—are too real and take the work of professionals. Your chosen friend must drive a nice car, sport a fashionable wardrobe, practice excellent grooming habits (weekly manicures are a must), and obsess about fitness.

The chosen friend must show good taste in wine, food, decor, movies, books, music, and, at least outwardly, men.

Second, must be a great talker. Your chosen friend must be willing to confess *everything* on a regular basis. Stoicism does not work here. No. What's needed is a real communicator, someone willing to hash over problems for hours.

Third, must be a terrible listener. Anyone ready to change the situation or behavior that created the resentment, anxiety, depression, or neurosis in her life should be eliminated from consideration as your chosen friend. The right candidate is so stuck in the muck that no pulling or prodding will get her out. She must be willing to do the same dysfunctional thing over and over, each time expecting different results. After all, friends who are ready to get on with things are like nonalcoholic beers. They don't taste right. And they definitely don't tickle your brain until it's numb.

Always remember that your conversations with this friend do not flow two ways. Do not waste time trying to get your friend to listen to *your* problems.

Fourth, must be a bit of a sleaze. Look for vices. You can't have a messy life without them. Nondrinkers (unless they are recovering alcoholics prone to relapse) and committed monogamists need not apply. Never shy away from a potential chosen friend who makes truth telling optional.

Fifth, preferred, but not mandatory, is a messy friend chosen from the workplace. That way, you can chew up hours and hours of *company time* in counseling sessions. The best friend for this job is one who regularly breaks down into crying jags throughout the day. It's a real bonus when the chosen friend is having an affair with another coworker. Wow. Talk about a rush. Picture it. She and your other coworker regularly go off for "lunch" and end up in a hotel room ripping each other's clothes off (or so you're told). But your other coworker is less committed to the affair than your friend. Maybe your other coworker harbors more guilt feelings regarding a spouse than your friend and can't really "perform" sufficiently. If you are lucky, the friend will blame herself for this lack of perform-ance, thinking she must not be attractive enough for your "nonperforming" coworker.

After lunch, she rushes to your office, shuts the door, and crumples into a fashionable ball of tears. As she tells you *all about it,* you will notice that your friend's collarbones are protruding and that you can see the veins in her arms. *(Of course, she's skinny. She spends her lunch hour trying to screw your other coworker.)* You also notice her perfect manicure.

Stay focused. Reassure her of her beauty and sex appeal. Offer a mild piece of advice you know she will not take, because you've offered it one hundred thousand times. That's okay. Remember, you don't really want her to get better.

Lastly, must be available for drinks. Make a date for you and your chosen friend to continue the conversation at happy hour. When that hour arrives, choose a place that serves margaritas in fishbowl glasses—the kind of glass you can almost dive headfirst into and swim around in, while your friend continues her lamentations. Every now and then, come up for air and begin musing about the reasons for your other coworker's "nonperformance."

"Maybe he's gay," you might say.

"Oh, God, you think?"

"I don't know. Maybe. Maybe he can't do it with his wife, so he's trying to do it with you. But he's really gay, so he can't do it with *any* woman."

"You think?"

"Maybe. Besides"—and you hold up your little pinky and comically wiggle it a few times—"what are you really missing? You said so yourself, right?"

This makes your friend laugh through her tears. Your work is done. You've been there for your friend. She has provided you with your little vicarious thrill. Now you can go home with any thoughts of your pathetic life muffled in an alcoholic buzz.

Bike Balm

FOR MY FORTY-EIGHTH BIRTHDAY, I bought a new bike, a Trek 720 with twenty-one gears and an extra-soft suspension seat—a low-tech machine that complements the natural world with its quietness and lack of fumes. It replaced my fifteen-dollar yellow yard-sale bone-shaker I'd bought six weeks before that steered stiffly, and badly needed new brakes and gears. Even so, with that poor thing, I could glide like an ice-skater in figure eights on St. Luke's School blacktop in west-central St. Louis, which reawakened an old feeling of euphoria I used to have years ago while biking. Riding at my age (now fifty-one) has made me feel many years younger and, most importantly, healthy again and more mobile. To enjoy that feeling even more (without straining some long-forgotten muscle and making the disability I have worse), I bought a decent machine, and found this well-designed, well-made bike a joy to ride.

It's burgundy-red with gold detailing, red like my very first bike, a J. C. Higgins balloon-tired flyer I inherited from my older brother. My father taught me to ride it the summer of

1957, when I had turned six. It was indestructible, the frame and rims being probably recycled World War II armor plating, making it too heavy for me to hold up and balance, and it was too tall to mount. Stepping up on a box, I would climb onto the seat, and gripping the handlebars very tightly, Dad would push me while he ran down the street, shouting: "Sit straight! Pedal! Pedal!" When I got up enough speed, he would give an extra shove and then let go, but I wobbled off only to crash, skinning my knees. He was a harsh teacher, not very patient. This wasn't to him a pleasant rite of a father teaching his child—rather, his approach was more like a boot camp sergeant—but his teaching me to ride the bike made this difficult man most like a father to me. One sultry afternoon, he let go for the last time, and I pedaled free. Feeling the fledgling's thrill of finding its wings at last, I laughed all the way as I soared past our neighbors' houses—Mrs. Mace's, the Pilgers', past Tommy, Joey, and Billy's—to round the curve at St. Stephen's Convent without spilling, past St. Stephen's School, and to the church. My speed did more than thrill me. I felt thoroughly alive, rocketing through the whole universe from my working-class neighborhood at South Third Street in Caseyville, Illinois. "Did you see me, Daddy? Did you see?" I shouted for the neighborhood to hear. "I did it!" I can still see him standing at the opposite end of the block with his hands on his hips, smiling.

From that moment, I loved bicycling. As a child, I gave

my bike mystic names (a new one for nearly every day), which I hung as a banner on its handlebars, dedicating it to all the fantastic, adventurous places I believed it would take me. Whenever I found a place where the dust was ankle-thick and powdery, I would pedal lightning fast at it, then jam on my brakes to rear and skid through it, stirring up dust devils so thick that the bike and I would be completely caked. At other times, I imagined the bike was the sleek, well-muscled black horse with flowing mane and tail I always wanted, and groomed it often with thick globs of smelly brown car wax, slathering its chain with 3 IN 1 oil. On our journeys, I even whispered to it words of encouragement or incantations to excite it to greater speed and daring, as I had watched the boy Ken on TV do for his friend Flicka.

One sweltering summer afternoon, I rode my bike on the street in front of my house in countless figure eights, turning and circling like a dervish in a trance. I couldn't seem to stop, though I was growing exhausted, my riding becoming clumsy and wobbly. I was vaguely conscious that my mother stood behind the front-door screen watching me, but she seemed light-years away and her call to me sounded as if it came from that distance. But those sound waves reached deep for me wherever I was, and in obedience, I awakened, and nearly falling off, I dismounted, dazed and nauseous, stumbling straight to bed without being told while it was still light. "It's too hot outside. Must be a hundred," she said. She sponged me down with a cold washcloth and then filled it with ice to put on my head. "Be careful, riding around when it's this hot. That's how you get polio." I fell into a fitful sleep under an oscillating fan, for it was as hot inside as it was outside, as few homes had air-conditioning in those days. I kept waking up to make sure I could still move my sore legs.

When I outgrew the red bike at age eleven, my family visited the same bike store where my brother's black three-speed racer that I coveted was bought three years before, to buy me a black Raleigh three-speed ladies' racer. It was Black Beauty with its gleaming fenders and chrome rims, an elegant and graceful machine that always stood "on pointe" like a ballet dancer and glided just as smoothly as we swept together in great figure eights or circles in the late-afternoon-to-twilight rides of summer. I would lean its slim, light frame as far as I safely could into each curve, feeling myself hovering just above the reach of gravity's pull, contacting the earth on only one inch of revolving rubber. Then, coming out of the curve, I'd straighten up to lean again in the other direction, swinging pendulum-like this way and that on the fulcrum of the tires' sidewalls. I rode fast or slow, according to some melody I always heard in my head, but my speed, choreographed as dance, made summer afternoons wind down like a music box. I usually found myself gliding about in a deep reverie, listening to the metronome tick . . . tick . . . tick of my gears as I pedaled, then to the sudden pizzicato of soft ticks that mimicked the cicada calls whenever I suspended pedaling to glide. The humid air of summer, which smelled of the sweet odor of mown grass and honeysuckle, blew on my face in my speed. As the evening approached, a cool haze hung in the shadows of the trees, drifting across the road I rode down. The evening air was still, except in my wake.

I did crazy biking, too, like the time in my early twenties when I rode thirty-five miles almost nonstop without water in ninety-five-degree, high-humidity weather. Why I did that, only heaven knows; sometimes I get this trekking bug that pumps gallons of adrenaline through me. During those times, I'm compelled to conquer mountains, ford great rivers, or ride these foolhardy trips in killer conditions. That day, I managed to get twenty miles before dizziness and muscle cramps set in, and suddenly my strength left me. I could only walk—or really stumble and weave—for the next five miles, being close to fainting a few times, before I could find a gas station with soda machines. A cold root beer fueled me for the next ten miles, but I was unable to make the return trip, as my knee gave out. This exercise in obsessive compulsion proved something, though. I now knew how to lose ten pounds in one day, evidencing that I also had lost my marbles somewhere along the way.

Bike riding in my older years can relive old thrills, so long as they're moderate. I notice now that I ride with my brakes on while going down hills, instead of zooming down them like a comet. Fast now really looks too fast, where in childhood, fast was never fast enough. I see that I don't lean into the curves nearly as sharply, either, as my balance isn't very good anymore. I can't go nearly as far, as fast, or as gracefully as I once did. Certainly, I don't ride around in furnace heat to test whether I'm immune to heatstroke. Age has given me some wisdom, but it can cost some in exhilaration. To tell the truth, I use the bike now as a disguised wheelchair, as I can't walk very far without encountering painful difficulty with my legs these days, the result of an illness. Sometimes, the loss of my athletic ability saddens me, but my bicycle rescues me from despair; with it, youthful speed and grace magically reemerge, making me immensely thrilled that I can still go somewhere on my own power.

And that gives me choices. Maybe today I'll cruise the mile to my favorite coffee shop or cruise from my Dogtown neighborhood in St. Louis to the shops on Delmar, a distance of two miles, one way. If I feel really adventurous, I'll board the commuter train with my bike for a trip east across the Mississippi to disembark at a much smaller town, where I don't have to compete for space on the bike trails. There, especially on a Sunday afternoon, I'll glide around lazily, having all of its sleepy downtown to myself. I'll weave my figure eights down the middle of Main Street, and feel every bit as much joy as that summer day in 1957. That's my way of aging gracefully—being the kid I was that day.

Nuts!

YOU CAN ALWAYS TELL when I've gotten into the Jif extra-crunchy peanut butter. Peer inside at the almost CD-sized surface of the spread of the forty-ounce jar, and it looks like a well-tended sand trap on a golf course: narrow, neatly raked rows and some scattered pebbles. That's because I eat my peanut butter straight out of the jar with a fork.

It's a ritual. I scrape off a small globule out of the jar, fork wide and one-third inch deep and one-third inch long. I let the smooth part melt in my mouth. (It's not called butter without reason.) After that, I proceed to chew on the bits of peanuts. I crunch one piece at a time between the canines, only on the right side.

Dr. Sullivan, my dentist, told me last visit that I've worn the enamel off the upper one. I tend to do this before I go to bed: some neurotic impulse, I imagine. Even at 190 calories per two-tablespoon serving, the health consequences have been, well, peanuts. It's the hungover feeling and peanut butter breath in the morning that get to me.

Gossip

WELL, THIS WAS YEARS AGO, but I'd heard from Mavis Springer (who had this tragic job editing a rag called *St. Louis Elegance*) that the developers of one of these ritzy new real-estate developments out in West County, named Pheasant Ridge or something, wanted to put a really classy ad in the *Post-Dispatch,* so they called up Howard Nemerov, who was U.S. poet laureate then, to ask him if he would write a poem to put in the ad, and Howard said he would, for $25,000. They couldn't deal with that, so Howard told them to call up this other, less famous poet, because he would probably do it, and they offered this young guy $1,000. He said no, but he made his wife, who was a model on a Kix box, write it, although as far as I know it was never in the paper.

Then I told that story to Gary Geary, who I went to grad school with. His poetry sucked, pardon my French, but he won a playwriting prize for a play making fun of Catholic school. They must have given him that prize for being so original. And then he got a job writing a column about how

St. Louis sucks, and was probably the most hated man in town; he got the filthiest hate letters, and even had J. C. Corcoran calling him Gary the Fairy on the air. Everybody I knew hated Gary, especially Paris Wycherly, because years ago he'd had a screaming fight with his girlfriend at one of Paris's themed champagne parties; but he'd never done anything to me, so I didn't hate him, which turned out good when he came back from Czechoslovakia, because Ray wanted to make him the editor of *St. Louis Elegance* after Mavis sued to get out of her contract. So I go in to see Gary, and congratulate him on his new job, and I hardly recognize him. He'd gained at least forty pounds; he's seven years younger than I am, and sitting there with silver hair and jowls like a mandrill. I'm in shock, and sitting there sweating because I don't know if he knows that his screaming ex-girlfriend, who couldn't get her novel published, went lesbian and then ended up getting shock treatment—Marty Olsen and I used to visit her and she didn't remember who we were—and she'd died, poor thing, of cardiac arrest from some med that kept her from rapid-cycling. I didn't know if Geary knew that, but I finally decided it wasn't my place to tell him, even though I thought her story might make a good article, "Death of a Nobody."

So, Geary just *has* to run pictures on the *St. Louis Elegance* celebrity pages of himself standing next to Chuck Berry. Then Geary quits, right, and I don't know it, so I write him an E-mail, and it's answered by the new editor, who's a woman—they always put a woman in charge when a rag is going broke—telling me that Geary quit and went to Scotland to write a book. And then the next month, this new editor phones and says that somebody that nobody knows had offered to do my column for fifty dollars a month. This editor asked me would I match the offer, and I said hell no, I don't take drastic cuts in pay. She says, are you sure you don't want to match the offer, and she was being so diplomatic that I got mad and said, when doves fly out of my ass, which was not what I should have said. The managing editor they'd had in the old days with Mavis, a girl we called Sherry Sardine, I'd liked her much better, although anything was better after we had that one editor we called Vlad the Impaler; I forget his name. Sherry used to work at *The Atlantic;* that's how you get a job in St. Louis. She wrote fiction, so I went to hear her read one of her stories about a woman who was, like, abandoned by her boyfriend and dead and in an imaginary room with four walls and no door, watching her boyfriend with another girl, and I thought to myself how embarrassed I was that when I was in that fiction-writing workshop with Tobias Wolff, I brought in short stories exactly like that, and I cringe just thinking about it, and how Toby must have cringed reading such crap. Oh, he was so nice. But not once, not once, did anybody ever tell me I ought to write nonfiction if I was so dead set on telling everybody the truth about how things really happened.

Dumpster Diving

A COUCH, faded and stained, is the first sign of the season. Dated in every aspect, it sits musty and abandoned in the alley. A few days later, a broken office chair, with rusted wheels and a torn vinyl seat, materializes. Soon, it will be one of a flock of such chairs. And then, finally, the ultimate harbingers of the season: discarded mattresses and box springs slumped against alley fences throughout my neighborhood.

Hallelujah! It's Dumpster diving time! Soon the alleys will be alive with people, me included, trolling for treasure in the trash.

I live near a university, whose students are—apparently—rather wealthy. As finals week and commencement approach, they begin to think about summer, and they begin to pack. More importantly, they begin to trash things they either don't have room for or don't want. This phenomenon peaks when they actually begin to load cars for the trip home.

Dumpster diving is a year-round avocation for some, pursued in the deep freeze of winter and the sultry days of summer. But I am a fair-weather diver. I limit my excursions to the high season, which starts about mid-April in my neighborhood and winds down in June, depending on graduation schedules.

Drivers in SUVs and minivans will eye one another jealously from opposite ends of the block, in a race to have first pickings in the debris surrounding an apartment-building Dumpster. Longtime residents will cast hostile looks at strangers scavenging everything from plastic milk crates to bedding to pieces of furniture.

We scavengers are a varied crew. There are the daily dog walkers, who take only what they can easily carry—except when they happen upon something great, in which case they hurry home, hoping the find will still be there when they return with a car. There are the casual coffee drinkers, who give the appearance they just happened to be poking around in the trash while out on a morning stroll. There are the professionals, armed with rubber gloves and golf clubs to allow for thorough exploration of particularly rich veins of cast-offs. These people drive oversized vans with roof racks and, occasionally, small trailers.

I was an occasional diver until I moved to this neighborhood. If I happened upon an attractive discard, I stopped to put it in the trunk of my car. Now—and this is the first I've admitted this—I'm verging on the fanatic. Not only do I scavenge for myself and friends, I can't resist things I don't need but that will certainly sell in my annual garage sale.

Neighborhood children beseech me to take them diving. "Yeah, 'cuz our mother said she wouldn't," lisped an eight-year-old after his eleven-year-old brother made the request. They were thrilled to score a weeping fig tree in a beautiful pot and—as the eleven-year-old excitedly told his mother—"a perfectly good Halloween decoration just sitting in the trash." And I've been leading others into temptation. Me, to a dog-walking-diver friend of mine: "Wanna go for a spin through the alleys?"

One year, I found a brand-new VCR, still wrapped in plastic in its box. A friend scored a Burberry raincoat, lightly used. An acquaintance went home with a stainless-steel laboratory trolley. Office chairs and bulletin boards and boom boxes are available in abundance. I've picked up so many of those lightweight, bagless vacuum cleaners that I have one in every closet.

My favorite find, though, was a box spring. My diving companion mentioned that she needed one for her guest room. We agreed this was one item we wouldn't pick up in an alley. Just then, a blonde coed and her equally blonde mother came out carting a very nice box spring. Hmmm.

"Would you mind if we took your box spring?" we asked.

"Oh, no. It's only two years old, but we don't have room to get it home," said the mother. "Do you want the mattress, too?"

"No, thanks. But would you mind helping us load the box spring?" (Chutzpah is a genetic requirement for Dumpster divers.) The mattress, by the way, was gone by noon.

As a recreational diver, I have my rules: (1) Don't go into the Dumpster. Take only what's on top or outside (or, in some cases, what's easily visible and just a few inches down). (2) Don't pick up anything that isn't perfect. Whatever it is will eventually come along in better shape. (3) Don't take what you don't need. Not only might someone else need it, your garage will soon fill up with detritus. This doesn't mean you can't hunt with the rest of us; I know one man whose wife won't let him bring anything home. He trolls anyway, stacking whatever he finds neatly alongside the Dumpster for the next diver. (4) Leave the alley cleaner than you found it.

What have the trash receptacles yielded? A crystal bowl, perfect for paperwhites in the spring. A set of leather luggage stacked to make a side table. A medicine cabinet for the basement bathroom. A collapsible picnic table that seats twelve. A Danish modern love seat and a hefty leather footstool. So many office chairs that I have a wide selection of spares in my garage.

We divers live by certain social rules, too. For example, don't start poking until the person who was at that Dumpster first is finished. And we cooperate. Once, my friend and I ran into a family of church women who had selected a dresser and bed from a pile of discards. But their car was too small, so one woman was going home for a bigger vehicle—leaving her elderly mother, in silk dress and hat, to guard the furniture. As it happened, there was a desk that wouldn't fit into my overly full car. The lady in the hat kept an eye on it—and had to vigorously discourage some latecomers who coveted it—until we emptied the car and came back

There are those, my former husband among them, who are disdainful of—or even disgusted by—the idea of taking something from the trash, let alone using it. On the other hand, he has been happy to accept a scrupulously clean blender and a brand-new coffeemaker whose exact origins he doesn't want to know.

My son used to groan and duck down in his seat when I turned into an alley while driving him to school. He once begged me not to make a beeline for a very nice folding chair that seemed to be the objective of a homeless man striding toward the same Dumpster. His attitude changed, however, the day we found a Swiss Army knife tucked into the cushions of an abandoned sofa.

Dumpster diving is hunting and gathering in its urban form. The thrill is in the discovery of the unexpected and in the knowledge of a particularly productive location. I used to satisfy my hunting urges at flea markets and garage sales, but those are too well picked over anymore. On-line auction sites have taken the fun out of scavenging by making it too easy—and too expensive. Dumpster diving is extreme shopping—meeting the challenge of finding something of value for nothing.

Television

THE VAST WASTELAND. The boob tube. Lowest common denominator. So true, but at my house, the TV is on.

Other than *The West Wing*, and before that *Homicide*, I watch few prime-time productions. I stick to reruns and syndicated shows. I never laughed at *Seinfeld*'s gang of four or *Night Court*'s ensemble until after the series concluded. I never saw Matlock wield his down-home charm or Angel sweet-talk Rockford into another scheme until their shows' third or fourth or eightieth go-round. What was the big deal about that Bart kid with the unlikely hair? Only in reruns did I discover that treasure trove of human behavior and emotions taken to the nth degree called *The Simpsons*.

Current favorites are *Murder, She Wrote* and *Duckman*. Critics panned *Murder, She Wrote*'s formulaic plots and over-the-hill actors. Still, I admire mystery writer Jessica Fletcher. Jessica never gets bent over weight, clothes, or some guy. She is polite but has the gumption to look someone in the eye and say, "No, Leslie, *you* killed him," and then rattle off exactly how and why. She's my hero.

Duckman is a cartoon duck whose uninhibitedly self-indulgent hedonism correctly relegates him to midnight on Comedy Central. The Duckman id sucks all into its vortex, including straitlaced porcine partner, Cornfed; Elvis look-alike nemesis, King Chicken; and his pathetically dysfunctional family. He is my hero, too.

Sleeping with a Married Man

THE FIRST TIME I saw him, my mind was devoid of thought. There was only the sudden knowledge that I had limbs and flesh, weight and height. Having always filtered the world through my mind or my heart, I had never had a purely physical reaction to anything, until then.

Whenever he looked or lingered, I experienced nothing but awkwardness. I was the little sister pest. It was as if I'd sprouted braces and pimples. I actually developed something of a stutter in his presence.

There was one night when I thought that he might be noticing me, too. A week later, it started. He called, invited, confessed. There was an exactness to the quality of his affection.

Except, of course, for the fact that he was married.

Since I lived alone, he was surely the one who had to invent more elaborate lies. Yet, seeing him was always a matter of whether he could sneak away, more often than not at the last minute, and I found myself canceling on almost anyone or anything with flimsy excuses. Just to be with him.

And then there was the matter of the unavoidable roller coaster of emotions and the string of lies, projecting the impression that nothing at all was new in my life. That I was not swooning, that I was not having fun, that I was not scared, that I did not feel special one moment and a fool the next.

Each embrace was clutching, each afternoon stolen. Risks and costs and gambles of all varieties. There were secrets to be kept and dramas to enact. In the inverted math that comes with being a mistress, this all made me feel very special—chosen.

I also felt tired.

Three months later, I went to a diner to breakfast with the one friend I'd told. She was wide-eyed for details, but I was confused and exhausted. I went home, shut the ringer off the phone, called in sick to work, and slept for three days. I let the machine get calls for a couple weeks more. His voice mails turned concerned, frantic, annoyed, angry, then resolute. He left his wife six months later for someone else.

On the Lam

I ASK, WHICH IS WORSE, to present myself as a nail-biting neurotic blaming her naughtiness on her inner child, who must still be acting up? Or as an adult who simply fesses up to having been wrong, sinful, or even wicked? What gets me more respect? Isn't it more dignified to stand up like an adult and point the finger at myself and say with all honesty, "The devil made me do it"?

How else can I explain what I did? An alien force invaded me. People get abducted by UFOs all the time—there's even support groups for such victims—so why not by Beelzebub? He's been around longer, and knows all the likely suckers to tempt, like me. The second I let my guard down, the old boy jumps inside and smacks around all my caution, my cultivated principles and good intentions, and then leaves me feeling guilty about not feeling guilty enough about having gotten away with whatever I did. Like the time last year a cop caught me on his radar going fifty in a thirty-five-mile-an-hour zone. I was in a tearing hurry to get somewhere unimportant and was paying no attention to road signs as I barreled through a ritzy neighborhood in west St. Louis with a dirty car, when suddenly a police car passes me going in the other direction. Immediately, my eyes click up to my rear-view mirror and I see him making a turn and coming right back in my direction. A wild suggestion coming out of nowhere told me to make a run for it—"Just keep driving, as if you didn't see him. Get over the crest of this hill and turn off onto a side street and ditch him." I obeyed like a slave.

It was a dead-end street I turned on, so I drove as far as I could, then sat waiting for the cop to drive by my hideout. It's a gleeful feeling to think you can elude the powers that be, but my euphoria didn't last but ten seconds, when I saw him turn onto my street. He caught me, of course, and he politely asked where I was going. *Do you live on this street?* I told the truth (sort of) that, no, I didn't live on that street, but when he asked, *Do you have some business being on this street?* I grew a little tongue-tied, then replied with my Oscar-winning, very audibly sighed exasperation act: "I'm lost." He looked doubtful but didn't argue and ticketed me only for speeding, charitably omitting my attempt to elude arrest. I felt bad that I was speeding. I felt bad that I had tried to escape. I felt even worse that I had lied. I felt chagrined, too, that I had to pay fifty bucks to the ritzy suburb, swelling the coffers of a community that needed the revenue the least, when I could have been speeding in an inner-city neighborhood. Guilt must be drunk to the dregs for full effect.

Although I feel appropriately guilty when I should, I don't know how to explain the sniggering sensation I relish when I think of the time I actually evaded the law and really did get away with something. It has to be the devil left his hoofprint in me from that occasion. A few years ago, I had tempted a nice, very law-abiding Jewish friend into trespassing with me onto derelict quarry property to explore the massive limestone cavern set in a huge bluff. "It's a fantastic place! The cave's a mile long and a quarter mile deep. It's filled with really old trucks and bulldozers covered really thick with dust. It looks like a mysterious ancient city. Don't worry about trespassing—the place's been abandoned for years. I've never been caught." My friend was intrigued, and especially desired to see the old highway equipment, the same as his quarry-owner grandfather had used in Missouri to build a section of old Route 66.

But someone spotted us sneaking into the cave's entrance and within two minutes, we heard the wail of a siren. My stomach grew queasy with fear as we ducked behind some boulders inside while the cop sped back and forth on the road in back of the cave, ordering us out with his bullhorn. He could have driven into the cave, but he didn't, nor did he get out to look for us, at least, not at that moment. As soon as he passed our position, I said to my friend: "There's no way I'm getting caught. Let's go!" and out we clambered through an opening at the back, and up the hillside we climbed through colonies of ticks, and chiggers, and waist-high poison ivy. We vanished into the thick brush in seconds, hoping our lawman wasn't that zealous to pursue us. The only escape route was to march over the ridge, up and down several ravines, slide down a steep bluff face, and tramp through a cornfield, a journey that would take four hours through junglelike vegetation. My friend began to assess our chances of escape:

"You know, he might be waiting by your car when we get back."

"Don't say that."

"What will we do if he's there?"

"Dunno. Wait him out, maybe. Surely he won't wait there all day."

"How much is the fine for trespassing?'

"Probably too much."

"Maybe he'll put us in jail overnight, just to put a scare in us."

I laughed nervously. "He has to catch us first. I'm not gonna do hard time."

I was upset I couldn't show my friend the cave and apologized to him profusely for leading him into this trouble, but soon we actually began to enjoy being on the lam, hiding in bushes, peeking around trees, peering over the bluff's edge. "A chill went down my spine—didn't it yours?—when that cop was buzzing us. It's a little taste of what it's like to be pursued. If that cop wasn't an overweight town constable, but instead a platoon of German soldiers, after us, we wouldn't be laughing right now. But we're here and not some other place in history, so might as well enjoy the hike!" At the end of our great trek and to our great relief, we found no one leaning against my car, which was parked at the town's deserted ball diamond, where most trespassers parked. We tore out of there and made good our escape.

Now, whenever my friend and I meet, we smirk at each other, being the apt thing to do knowing we feel guilty as hell over having gotten away with it, and yet feel foolishly good about it. But mostly, plain foolish.

Drinking

I LOVE TO DRINK. Red wine or margaritas, but other things will do. Gin-and-tonics are excellent. For all my practice, I don't hold my liquor very well. I get loud and silly. The next day I always, always, feel terrible. A piercing headache, a sloshing stomach, and the memory of flirting with someone I shouldn't have. Embarrassment quickly turns to shame. I count out the alcoholic calories and think what a nice meal I could've had instead. I swear I'll never do it again.

But then in a month or two, it'll be a hard day. I'll feel tired or angry or bored. Maybe even just annoyed. The first drink doesn't even taste right and I tense up with the thought of how stupid it is to be drinking. The second one makes me feel lighter and more social, tingly. From there, it's hard to gauge and my only hope is that someone else will want to call it an early night.

Being Right

————◦━◦━————

"SEE? I'M RIGHT!" Those are the three little words I most like to say. My whole life, I've needed to be right. All the time. About everything. And before anyone else blurts out the answer. Being right triggers not one, but two, positive feelings. One is the satisfaction a person feels when the right jigsaw piece nestles in its slot—a confirmation of one's worldview. The other is the rush of competition—I like to win.

I come by this trait honestly. When Mom would discover an interesting tidbit or a better way to do a task, she would share this with us in quiz form. "What is the link between James Arness of *Gunsmoke* and Peter Graves of *Mission Impossible*?" (They were brothers.) "What is the secret of making a whiter *bao ze* or Chinese steamed bun?" (Use pastry flour.) My sister and I eagerly entered this game with Mom and raced each other to give the right answer. Picking the tenderest green beans, folding socks so they were easy to put on, doing the elementary backstroke, all provoked the "I've got a secret; can you guess it?" smile from Mom.

This drive to be right has stood me in good stead. All through school, I shone. "What's the capital of Uruguay?" "I know. I know. It's Montevideo." "What is the most abundant chemical in the earth's atmosphere?" "I know. It's nitrogen." "I know. Kublai was Ghengis's grandson." "Mary Tudor, not Mary Stuart." "House Un-American Activities Committee." On standardized tests, I wielded my No. 2 pencil like a weapon.

Even in medical school, especially in medical school, I was rewarded for this trait. "I know. That painful spot in her neck and her fatigue point to subacute thyroiditis." "Hemachromatosis causes abnormal liver functions and severe arthritis." "Diabetes insipidus." "Type IV RTA."

I became an internist. The other residents called us *fleas* because they perceived us as nit-picking over minutiae and esoterica. "Did you check a free T4 by equilibrium dialysis?" "Given the symptoms and the patient's hepatitis C antibodies, I diagnose cryoglobulinemia." (We defended ourselves by accusing the surgical residents of adhering to the motto: "When in doubt, cut it out.")

It's only now, with my reading-glasses-assisted hindsight, that I see how obnoxious I must have been to others and how deeply lurked the fear of ever being wrong. Habits of a lifetime do not break easily, or even bend. I can sometimes not give away the joke punch line or the movie ending (although I am tempted), but I still break out in an embarrassed sweat when I find out something I've said isn't right.

Finding Tennis Heaven

EVERY FRIDAY, as my coworkers turn on their computers, take their first urgent phone calls, and pop their first diet Cokes, I start my negotiated three-day weekend with a leisurely drive up a winding forest-lined road. I arrive at the manned front gate of Principia College and cruise slowly past the guard who waves me in. I proceed down a lane under a cascade of sugar maples that in the fall make me realize why the color gold is in nature. I turn and follow the drive to the parking lot of pristine indoor tennis courts. I call it Tennis Heaven.

Inside, Ed, Colin, Nikki, maybe Jerry or Jack or Emilio, call out effusive greetings. "There she is," "She made it." "Come, warm up with us."

They are retired faculty and long-ago students of this, the only Christian Science college in the world. Ed, the organizer of our little morning tennis clan, is well past eighty. Yet, he plays almost every day. In the six years that I have been playing here, he has worn the same blue sweater vest at the beginning of every match and his game has not slipped. He still has the same tricky little angle shots and wicked, spinning drop shots that used to frustrate me and have forced me to learn to bend my knees and stay patient. Ed also has the same twinkle in his eye. And, once in a while, he will pop off a flirty little comment.

"I've been waiting for those legs to arrive," he might say. Or, when I tell him I can't play again until the next week, "I will be waiting with bated breath."

From the moment I take to the court, all thoughts of the work I'm missing fall away. That I take an extra day off each week for the stated purpose of pursuing another college degree, *not* for improving my forehand, is okay with me, too. My theory is that the world would be better if we all had a three-day weekend. So, this is my sacrifice for society's benefit.

Colin and Nikki, now retired, travel the world. They might spend a month of the winter in Maui. They might take up spring residence in Tuscany, where Colin can practice his Italian and write poetry. But when they are home, they, too, play daily morning tennis.

Colin serves a low skidding ball that will slide past me if I am not quick and agile enough. And while I can often execute a passing shot at Nikki's feet, she can best me with a forehand return that stays low, angles sharply, skims the line, and hits the side curtain before I can get my racket on it.

As for the rest of our group, well, I never rush the net on Jerry, Ed's wife. She will put up a perfect lob that soars over my head and lands—without fail—squarely on the back line. And she will smile the whole time. Jack, also a retired professor, has an ever-affable nature that keeps me from being annoyed when he poaches a ball I have returned. Emilio runs down every ball with what I imagine to be the same gusto he used as a boy on the soccer fields of his native Argentina.

Collectively, these are the nicest people I have ever known. I am not a Christian Scientist, so I have no affiliation with Principia College. Yet, six years ago, they welcomed me into their group by virtue of the fact that I lived in a neighboring village and happened to play tennis. In that time, I have never paid for court time. It is completely free to them, so it is completely free to me. Even better, I can count on one hand the negative comments I have heard—about anything. They demonstrate a genuine concern for the affairs of the world, yet each remains infectiously positive. And while I don't think I could ever follow a religion that does not consider medicine an option for healing (I love my Prozac way too much), I suspect the serenity I have witnessed in this group stems from that very spiritual base. Every time I play with these people, I feel grateful that I took up this fickle game.

I didn't start playing tennis until age thirty-two. My first motivation in seeking out the summer tennis clinics at a nearby park—and in purchasing my first short white tennis skirt— was to meet men. I quickly learned the folly of that expectation. First of all, most of my tennis clinic classmates were women. The few men who came to those clinics were one of two types. Either they were there to meet women—but women in size 4 tennis skirts, not my size 8 tennis skirt (and those who would settle up, I would not settle for)—or they were the type whose awkward shyness kept them from even wanting to meet women, so they had plenty of time for tennis.

Ever determined, I started a brief relationship with one of the tennis clinic's instructors, who also turned out to be one of the most screwed-up individuals I have ever met in my life. While we were dating (and I use the term loosely), Brad (I'll call him Brad) remained preoccupied and enmeshed with an equally crazy ex-wife, habitually slept with his children's baby-sitter, and carried on some kind of relationship that never was clear to me with a recently divorced neurotic woman who drove a Lincoln and looked suicidal.

At forty-something, Brad did not have a checking account. And, with the exception of the nights he spent with one of the above lucky females or on the couch of his chronically ill parents, he slept in his car. Brad was homeless, had no insurance, no savings, nothing. What a catch, huh? I did manage to score some free tennis lessons before someone with better legs and a more neurotic penchant for fucked-up men squeezed me off his social calendar.

By that time, I was ready to move on to the world of USTA tennis. This meant joining a team of players who practiced with a coach once a week to get ready for a Sunday match against a team that represented another tennis club. I played in this format for about five years. Each year, the tennis got more competitive. And, each year, the women I played with got crazier.

I describe my last team in USTA tennis as a band of laughing hyenas. You only have to watch a nature show for a few minutes to realize that one minute hyenas can be happily rolling around on their backs, legs kicking playfully in the air, and the next minute they can be tearing the head off a poor gazelle. That describes my last USTA tennis team and the intrepid Mildred and Myrtle, who led us to sorrowful defeat or even more sorrowful victory each week. Mildred and Myrtle (I'll call them Mildred and Myrtle) preferred to play together. They liked each other's cutthroat competitiveness and wily style. The rest of us preferred it, too, because they were too loud, opinionated, and judgmental for anyone to survive the match. Unfortunately, it didn't always work out that way.

During my last match with my last USTA tennis team, my partner, Myrtle, scowled when I lost my serve, yelled at me for missing an overhead, and, on the third time in a row that I hit the opponent's serve into the net, rudely announced it was the third time in a row that I hit the opponent's serve into the net. At the end of the match, which we lost in two decisive sets, I refused to shake my partner's hand (a huge faux pas in tennis) and stormed out of the shabby tennis club we called home, never to return.

Let others pull out their checkbooks every Sunday to put up with shrieking menopausal lunatics who can't stand to lose. I prefer to serve them up gently in congenial, no-pressure, no-pay Tennis Heaven.

"When can you come again," Ed always asks.

"Soon. I hope. Very soon."

Girl Mechanic

I RECEIVED in the mail yesterday the latest catalog from Lindsay Publications, a publisher that sells "unusual technical books, past and present, of exceptionally high quality revealing skills and secret processes almost forgotten." The industrial basics that paved the path to contemporary life revealed step-by-step, and lavishly illustrated—all heady stuff for someone hungry to know what makes things go, how things are made. Here at work as a mechanical drafter (please note—not drafts*man*), I've been stealing glances through this catalog, searching for the book that most completely details the evolution of modern technology from the steam age or earlier. Some good reprinted manual from my grandparents' generation that might guide me if my computerized world can't be switched on. You just never know these days what'll happen. Perhaps the only reliable power is knowledge.

Modern Steam Engines, by Joshua Rose, M.E., jumps out at me. The catalog says that "Rose was a stellar engineer of his day" (late nineteenth century). My mind's eye sees his tintype visage wearing bushy sideburns, his right hand clasping his tweed coat lapel, looking every decimal inch or millimeter the engineering conqueror, gazing, as he might, squarely at the camera, exuding Victorian progress-will-prevail confidence. This mental picture gives me a needed shot in the arm, living as I have through half of the angst-filled twentieth century, and God knows how many years I have yet to live in the vulnerability of the twenty-first. The caption features a few samples of the beautiful 1887 hand engravings in the book, tempting me to buy it just for its patent-drawing art. (Nobody draws that way anymore.)

Yes, I'm tempted, but then Dave Gingery's *The Charcoal Foundry* and its sequel, *The Metal Lathe,* jump off the page. Dave promises that the first book will show me how to build a foundry for less than twenty-five dollars that is capable of melting enough aluminum to make his lathe for less than fifty dollars. From there, I could use his "simple lathe to build the metal shaper, milling machine, drill press, and the fancy accessories." He's implying that I'd have a whole machine shop, ready to fashion the nuts and bolts of modern life. It looks like a lot of physical work, though. So I page onto *Sundials, Their Theory and Construction,* by Albert Waugh. The caption promises that not only can I learn to construct polar, analemmatic, equatorial, and many other sundials, projects that upper-body weaklings like myself can perform, but it will even show me how to find the time for any location, even from moonlight. If I'm a castaway on a deserted island, bereft of watch escapements or digital microcircuits, I can still maintain modern frenzy and arrive on time to the beach or coconut-grove activities.

Lindsay's catalog has a few things to interest women, such as *Build Your Own Earth Oven* and *Cooking with the Sun* and *Making and Using Dried Foods,* but mostly this catalog is emphatically male. Some of Lindsay's books appeal to an adult male's adolescent streak and sexual immaturity, as in *Backyard Ballistics*—"a crazy book for little boys who never grew up and still want to get into trouble," detailing how-to with a potato cannon or tennis-ball mortar made out of PVC pipe. "Ram a potato up its orifice [I think it's called the muzzle], spray a little hair spray in the back end, and set that sucka off!" says the caption. Once my engineering boss had the model-shop guys construct (on company time) a potato cannon. "I fired an Idaho nearly seventy-five yards! You shoulda seen the muzzle flash. Two feet long! French fries to go!" Being technically minded, I listened carefully to my giggling boss describing the roaring, perhaps deadly, effect produced by the cannon's primitive design, but being a woman, I felt the potato had sadly missed its true target on a dinner plate. I, too, can enjoy the beauty in ballistics—the graceful parabolic trajectory—but isn't a baked potato, its casing split by a knife (rather than exploded into a tree) and its fluffy white insides smothered with broccoli-cheese sauce, lovelier still? I didn't care that he was my boss—someone had to respond to male foolishness and say: "Didn't your mother tell you it was a sin to waste food?" It's what my mother would have said, and her mother. He giggled even harder, this time at me, as if he were a boy having found yet another barbaric and completely outrageous male prank (more fun than earthworms or crawdads ever were) to horrify the sensibilities of the girls.

It all worries me—how things work, how they are made. Ignorance is not bliss; it's vulnerability. Whether we're male or female, we think, breathe, talk, technology whether we bake bread in our bread makers or run a giant factory. Perhaps, then, all of us should be hardwired, knowing intuitively everything about how things go, why they work; but most of us—male or female—don't. I know I lag several millennia behind in understanding the how and why, and I don't like the feeling. Is it because I didn't go to engineering school or get shop classes in high school, or is it because technology itself made me lazy? It doesn't help that someone's discovering new technologies every day, leapfrogging over old ones until I can't see what basis formed the modern conveniences I am forced to use, as obsolete ways pass out of living memory. Already, I've met young folks who've never used a rotary-dial phone. Another skill lost.

I like to blame most of the ignorance on the invasion of electronics. I don't like electronics because its functions are mysterious—not like mechanics, which can be figured out by simply watching drive trains crank long enough. Like mechanics, electronics make things go, but the problem for me is that it does it secretly. For every mechanical device replaced by an electronic one, there is a gain in speed and accuracy, along with sleeker, more trouble-free designs, but the trade-off is that it ties life to a wall plug, power grids, world politics. It increases mechanical ignorance, so that when the power goes out, there you sit in the dark without heat or air-conditioning. Like survivalists, I have always distrusted electronics. It makes me feel more defenseless, and do I need more of that? A woman always feels vulnerable in a man's world, and on top of that, these days nobody's mother teaches you how to sew, can food, or churn butter. Just thinking about being a twenty-first century woman sets my nerves on edge.

I turn to a page in Lindsay's catalog to *The Voice of the Crystal,* by Pete Friedrichs. It's about primitive electronics, but maybe I should get this. The caption reads: "Pete will take you a cut above the average crystal set builder by showing you how you can BUILD a crystal detector . . . BUILD headphones . . . BUILD capacitors . . . and all the rest and create a functioning radio." All I'd have to do to make a good radio is to scrounge some copper wire, mailing tubes, and tin cans, and have just enough mechanical moxy to put it all together.

Even I can do this. Already, I feel a surge of power just thinking about it.

Being a Bohemian

MY LACK OF COMMITMENT is always what I beat myself up with during anxiety or depression: no career, no spouse, no children. Secondary torture concerns my lack of money, educational degrees, artistic recognition, or anything that resembles success.

But my lack of an anchor can also be the source of a deep, rich pleasure. I look around at my life sometimes and think, "My God, I've outsmarted them all. I've gotten by with something—something *huge*."

I've managed an adult life in which I seldom follow anyone's orders. And where the only considerations I have to weigh are my own.

Like a miser playing with a pile of gold coins, I revel in earning the smallest amount of money possible to maintain independence and circumvent any true financial hardship.

In a melancholy mood, an aimless weekday can spiral down into feelings of profound and sweeping failure. But I have often spent a whole day reading a novel, watching the weather through my huge windows, eating and sleeping when the impulses strike. It feels, then, like I've found a secret passageway. And I can't believe the good fortune, instinct, or intellect that's brought me here.

Using The Bad Word

I WAS BORN CUTE.

I was a cute child and a cute college student. It's possible that one day I will be a cute crone. I can't shake it. But I can dilute its impact. The fastest way is by using The Bad Word.

I love The Bad Word. I love that crude syllable shot straight to the bull's-eye.

I love the thunk when it hits the target, dead on.

I love its blunt, Anglo-Saxon pedigree. I love its satisfying impact, challenged only by "hockeypuck"—which is useless, as it lacks The Bad Word's outlaw thrill.

Most of all, I love its effect on me. With The Bad Word, I become whatever I please. A gangster moll. A radical feminist. A CEO tossing down a martini. A cowgirl roping doggies.

The liberty of emphatic speech! The power of using all the words at my command, every shade of lipstick in the makeup kit, even that blaring shameless blood-red one, smearing it across the mirror.

I mean it.

I, am, not, kidding.

%#@!! you.

%#@!! off.

What the %#@!!.

No %#@!!ing way.

What do you mean, the nation has a $145-%#@!!ing-billion-dollar budget deficit? What happened to the surplus?

The Bad Word belongs to the highest echelon of words—those that sound like what they mean. I see them on display in a crystal case, lighted for effect: Sidle. Waddle. Crunch. Truculent. Sibilant.

On a shelf of its own sits The Bad Word, that clenched fist, that guttural punch, that ticket out of the cuteness cage.

I was twenty-seven, small and quiet. The company president, who had never promoted a woman, called me into his big office to explain why he couldn't promote *me*. Of course, he didn't have to say it. I knew exactly what the problem was. He thought I was cute.

"I can't walk around on eggshells. My managers have to take what I dish out! What if I called you in here and really let you have it? You'd cry, for God's sake."

I shrugged. "I'd say, 'Larry, go %#@!! yourself.'"

And I got the job.

Burning Bridges

I AM JUST NOW, in midlife, learning to live in the middle of things. Not that I like it. The light is dim here in the middle, the pace slow, the pulse-raising events few and far, far, far between. It feels sticky, uncomfortable, often suffocating. Those who say things say that the way to happiness is to find some sort of inner light in this murky middle. My head knows they are right. But my heart says, "Let's get this over with and move on."

I much prefer to begin things—start a new project, move to a new neighborhood, get a new job, begin a new essay. Beginnings are luminous, full of promise, mystery, and excitement. With something new to focus on, I shift my heart into fifth gear and propel myself down a new road yelling "yeeee-haaaa" all the way.

Of course, blazing new starts require endings, fiery ones. To be able to give my attention to brand-new projects, jobs, relationships, I've always found it helpful to throw out the stale, less exciting projects, jobs, relationships, along the roadside, allowing them to break apart as they bounce and clang in my wake.

As an undergraduate twenty-something years ago, I began the spring semester of my senior year with the intention of finishing solidly. After starting my college career with enthusiasm, gusto, and straight A's, I lost my way somewhere around my sophomore and junior years and limped along doing what I had to do to stay above a C average. But feeling the end coming, I decided to kick it in for a final blast of satisfying scholastics. My most important class of my final semester was a newspaper-writing course. I wrote three stories in the first week and received high praise for them all. This kind of productivity continued until the weather got nicer and the cold beer started tasting even better. In the last three weeks of classes, I failed to turn in one word to my assignment editor. I also failed to count up the number of stories I had turned in and didn't realize it wasn't enough to pass the course. My editor, clearly disappointed in me, gave me the grave news. It didn't matter how good my features were, I would not pass the course (and graduate) because I had shorted her and the paper by three stories. Devastated and ashamed, I literally fell to my knees and begged this professor to pass me with a C. I don't know why—and looking back I realize it would have been better for me if she hadn't—but she begrudgingly agreed. I left her office and got very drunk.

People who say things advise us not to burn our bridges.

When I hear that, I wonder if they have ever really tried it. I doubt these wiseacres have ever experienced the sheer rush and anticipation of pouring that kerosene, lighting that match, and running to the seeming safety of the next stage in life. I say there is really no better way to make a final statement, to have the last word, to end it, than to burn a bridge. Sure there's some remorse on the other side. But can't that be easily assuaged by taking in the freshness of this greener, unspoiled grass?

I once left a perfectly good job in a solid, if rather staid, corporation to work in the artsy environs of a chic, fashionably gray-toned (it was the eighties) graphic design firm. The first day—after settling into my windowed office with its walnut desk and credenza—I sped off in the backseat of the firm's owner's red BMW convertible with him and my boss. We were off to visit an important client. Even though the owner addressed me by the wrong name, I thought I had died and gone to heaven. I was suddenly a creative maven with my hair blowing in the wind (and in my face).

It didn't take long for the shine to wear off this scene and for my relationship with this owner to tarnish into blackness.

I became a terrible employee. I spent hours on the telephone with personal calls, took long lunches with coworkers, and gave the work I was given scant attention. I felt completely justified in this behavior, of course, because everyone knew that this person we all "slaved" for was a *deceitful, misogynistic womanizer.* He lied so often, he didn't know what the truth was anymore. Wearing my misery like a coat of arms, I stomped into work every day for three years—just long enough to save enough money to start my own freelance business. Then, I was congratulated for being so bold and so brave. Friends threw me a new-business shower. I got calls of encouragement. Old clients (of his) gave me work to get me started. I was on to something new. And I never had to look back on the great big mess I left behind. Now, that's a great beginning.

And this, I've just decided, is the end.